Taking Off

Taking Off

By JOANNE E. BERNSTEIN

Illustrated by KATHIE ABRAMS

A Harper Trophy Book

Harper & Row, Publishers

The author gratefully acknowledges permission to reprint the following material:
Page 12–13, adapted from *The Traveling Woman* by Dena Kaye, copyright © 1979 by Dena Kaye. Used by permission of Doubleday & Company, Inc. Page 149, from Macmillan Illustrated Almanac For Kids by Ann Elwood, Carol Orsag and Sidney Solomon. (Copyright © 1981 by Ann Elwood, Carol Orsag and Sidney Solomon.)

The illustrator wishes to thank the following for their generous help with reference material: Trans World Airlines, Amtrak, Trailways, the New York Public Library, the Port Authority of New York, American Youth Hostels, Marjorie Winogrond of Leeway Travel, and the friends who helped with foreign languages.

Taking Off

Designed by Trish Parcell
Published in hardcover by J.B. Lippincott, New York
First Harper Trophy edition, 1986

Library of Congress Cataloging in Publication Data
Bernstein, Joanne E.
    Taking off.

    Bibliography: p.
    Summary: A collection of travel tips for teenagers who are learning how to travel on their own.
    1. Travel—Juvenile literature. [1. Travel]
I. Abrams, Kathie, ill. II. Title.
G151.B485 1986   910'.2'02   85-45171
ISBN 0-397-32107-4 (lib. bdg.)

    "A Harper trophy book."
ISBN 0-06-446047-9 (pbk.)   85-45440

To Robin and Andy,
taking off and going full speed

Contents

Contents

Introduction

Last summer, 16-year-old Anthony traveled by bus from
Toledo, Ohio, to Cheyenne, Wyoming, to visit his father.
He slept on the bus one night and in a hotel the other. For
half a day on the bus he sat next to a woman from New
York. She told him that frequently in baseball season the
top of the Empire State Building is bathed in blue and
white lights, in honor of New York's home team, the Yan-
kees.

Before her junior year, Robin signed up for an American Youth Hostels bicycle tour of the Oregon coast. She
saw some of the best scenery the United States has to
offer, learned how to tighten a ten-speed gearshift lever,
and was taught how to make music with ordinary kitchen
spoons by a folksinger in the Cannon Beach hostel.

Both Anthony and Robin traveled on their own. So did

1

Jennifer, who flew 1,000 miles to take a biochemistry course at the University of Indiana, and Russell, who went backpacking with friends in Vermont's Green Mountains.

If you've outgrown traveling with your family and are headed for a trip on your own, planning is the key to success. *Taking Off* is a guidebook for getting around away from home.

You can use *Taking Off* in the United States and abroad. Whether you are thinking of spending a weekend 20 miles away or taking a trip across the country, *Taking Off* will help. You'll find out:

- why travel agents don't charge for their services
  (see p. 100)
- three hints for traveling with a friend to ensure that the friendship continues after the trip
  (hints on pp. 12–15)
- how to find the lowest airfare, and perhaps even how to fly free
  (see pp.17–24)
- what to do if you run out of money in Peoria
  (see pp. 147–48)

Do you want to know how to . . .

- get a passport?
  (step-by-step instructions are on pp. 106–9)
- pack your favorite shirt without wrinkling it?
  (there's a diagram on p. 132)
- get the most out of a theme park visit?
  (see suggestions on pp. 82–83)

- spend a night at a Y?
  (learn how on p. 71)
- choose the best backpack for a camping trip?
  (tips are on pp. 127–29)
- buy traveler's checks?
  (money matters are discussed on pp. 110–13)
- get a bus ticket that's good for a month of unlimited travel?
  (the procedure is described on p. 39)
- beat travelers' blues?
  (ideas for getting over homesickness can be found on pp. 139–40; strategies for meeting people appear on pp. 144–47)

Taking Off is a book about all aspects of travel, from how to reserve a motel room to how to stay safe and well on the road. Use the table of contents and index to find what you need to know for your trip.

Good traveling!

1. Getting Ready

Can we all go on the same trip and be happy? Probably not. Andrew rushes toward a mountain camping trip with great excitement, but Todd prefers to lounge on a beach. Amy dashes away for a month or longer, and Leah likes to come home after four or five days. One person may want to get away with no set schedule, while another may need to know where every moment will be spent. Your ideal trip may mean going it alone, going with one friend, or traveling with half the senior class.

Whatever your preferences may be, you're more likely to have a good time if you have certain personality traits. A Maupintour brochure states it this way: "Travel necessitates being a good-natured realist, as well as a romantic, and requires an agreeable acceptance of situations as they exist, not as each of us might prefer them to be. A pleasant tolerance makes for an enjoyable travel experience. If you are this appreciative traveler, you'll have the time of your life!"

Travel writer Dena Kaye tells it this way: "To travel is to take a journey into yourself. The truths uncovered may not always be pleasant. You must face your own preferences, strengths, and quirks—and live with them (and sometimes subject others to them). Without the bunting of a daily routine and familiar faces, you almost have to find yourself in every new environment. In uncharted situations, you are forced to call on your instinct and common sense for guidance."

Being open to unexpected situations and new aspects of yourself is as helpful on your fiftieth trip as it is on your first, but you can make every trip enjoyable if you ask yourself questions and think things through in advance.

How Long Should You Be Away?

The answer to this question depends upon your purposes for traveling. A *Psychology Today* survey found six different reasons for taking vacations: to relax and relieve tension; to learn something; to visit with family and friends; to have an exotic adventure; to find oneself; and to escape.

If you can identify your reason for going away, you may have a tentative answer for how long you should stay away. How much time do you need to rest up after the tensions of final exams? How many days does it take to learn to sail? To master first-term calculus? To become a fairly competent potter? If you're visiting relatives, is what people say about fish and visitors true—that they both begin to smell after three days? How much do you want to see? Your answers to these and other questions will help you set a time frame for your trip.

Another deciding factor should be your past experiences being away. Think back. If you've been away for several weeks at a time—at camp, in school, or visiting— how has it worked out? What about the times you've been away for only a few days? Which trips have been better for you? You may decide to stay with the pattern you've already enjoyed or you may want to try out something different, but going over your trip history can help you get ready.

Generally speaking, you will probably be happiest if you change your pattern gradually. If you've been away before for a few days or a week, and now you want to go away for a longer time period, it's smart to try out a two- or three-week trip before signing up for a nine-week jaunt.

The same is true for distance. Most travelers do not fly off for Europe until after they get practice closer to home. Your first trip may be only an hour from home. You may have to take several trips a few hours away from home before you're ready for a trip that takes you two days' traveling time.

How far you should go and how long you should stay away will depend on one other factor: how much money you have. Sit down with pencil and paper and add up the tentative costs for the vacation you have in mind. With the help of the sources discussed in this book, figure out how much each breakfast, lunch, and dinner is likely to cost you, how much a night's lodging will be, and what you must set aside for getting to your destination and back.

Stick to a trip that you can pay for. There is usually no opportunity to earn money away from home. Plan a trip with enough money to get there, to live comfortably each day, and, MOST IMPORTANT, to get home.

Should You Have a Schedule?

Some people travel with every hour planned out—they may know where each night will be spent, where each meal will be eaten. Others travel with next to nothing planned—they may know only their arrival and departure dates.

How much you plan out your trip in advance will depend upon what your goals are and what makes you most comfortable. Think about why you're going away. Will a set schedule help or hurt? If your purpose is to relax, will knowing where you have to go next relieve tension for you? Or will following an itinerary be a pain in the neck?

Setting your itinerary in advance has advantages:
- You can pay for lodging in advance and know that a room is waiting for you.
- By reserving your sightseeing tours before you leave, you will not waste time searching for activities.
- You will know almost to the penny how much a trip will cost.

There are disadvantages, though.
- If you find you've stuffed too much or too little into each day, you are still bound to the agreements you've made and may have to rush around madly or be bored waiting for the next activity to begin.
- You are not free to make changes if you find something else you'd rather do or someplace else you'd rather stay, and, if an emergency forces you to change your plans, you'll likely have to pay anyway.

A good compromise between the two extremes might be:
- Having a confirmed lodging reservation for your first night away.
- Reserving a room for your first night in any place that is a top tourist attraction.
- Reserving a room for your first night in any town where a festival or celebration will be going on.
- Carefully figuring out how many miles you can comfortably travel in a day.

- Breaking your trip into two or three parts, planning varied activities and perhaps a highlight for the middle of the vacation.

No matter how much you schedule, it's never possible to see everything. Here's an idea that may give you a sense of accomplishment: Choose one particular focus area for sightseeing on each trip. An example might be architecture. In Tulsa you'd make sure to see the wonderful Art Deco buildings, and in San Francisco you'd be on the lookout for colorful Victorian homes. This might make it less painful to miss some of the museums.

Traveling Alone or with Companions

Will you go on your trip alone? With a relative? With a friend? How about two friends? Three?

There are advantages to traveling alone, and disadvantages as well. Likewise, there are both good and bad points about traveling in a pair or as part of a larger group.

What can be said for solo trips? You set the pace. You eat when *you* are hungry, sleep when *you* are tired, and no one drags you around castles when you've already seen more than your share.

When you travel alone, any accomplishment or discovery is all yours. And even when you are lonely or get into trouble, once you've solved the problems, you feel good about yourself and what you've learned you can do.

Decisions are made faster when you are on your own. Traveling alone forces you to find your way, and you're more likely to soak in the local culture. You can still meet new people. Waiters and hotel staff know where young people get together and can direct you to roller rinks, beaches, town squares, and other gathering places.

Why travel with company, then? If you want to share the day's events right then and there, you can do it. If something marvelous happens (the sudden appearance of a rainbow, for example), you have someone to shout to, "Wow, look at that!"

Traveling with a companion gives you a larger pool of ideas. You may get dragged to an extra museum now and then, but you also have two brains to figure out what to do if the car runs out of gas.

A trip with company usually means lower costs for each person. A motel room for a single occupant might cost $30. The same room, shared by two, may cost only $36, and the rate may be $38 for three. If you are alone, you pay the whole $30. Go with a friend and your share is about $18. Go with two friends, and you sleep for under $13. Multiply this by two weeks, and you've saved a bundle.

Going on a trip with friends gives you the mixed blessing of getting to know them better. You will probably see character traits and habits in your friends that you never noticed before, no matter how long you've been acquainted. Some will be annoying ("I never knew Jim took so long in the bathroom"), while others may be endearing ("Did you know Jim could plan a budget that never runs over?").

A trip gives you and your companions something to share together. Before you go, you can discuss your plans. Afterward, you can reminisce about the trip.

How to Choose a Travel Companion

You must choose a travel partner very carefully, bearing in mind that you will share close quarters. Neither of you will be able to keep your usual defenses up for very long; both your good and bad moods will show through. Normally, in the course of a day, our needs are met by lots of different people. On a trip, you will be called upon to meet more of your partner's needs, and your partner will have to respond to yours. This may mean anything from waking a late sleeper, or listening to old camp stories, to taking someone to a hospital.

If you think you might get along well with your friend or cousin, discuss as many aspects of the trip as possible before making a commitment. Dena Kaye, author of *The Traveling Woman*, recommends answering a few questions together. She stresses that it's important to be honest with yourself and your prospective companion.

Her first question is a fill-in: "I'm going on this trip because . . ." You should both agree on your basic purpose. If one of you wants to have adventures, but the other wants to rest up on the beach, you may not be the best match.

Kaye's next question checks on mutual interests. "Describe a perfect day and a perfect night." What time do you get up? What do you do then? What do you plan to do for each hour of the day? You needn't be matched up identically here, but your wake-up time, bedtime, energy level, and activities should be fairly similar. If you're going to run from morning until night, you'd both better like it. You can overcome small differences, but not large ones.

More questions: What kind of lodging do you like? What kinds of people do you like? What kinds of food? Entertainment?

Still more: How much do you want to spend? How will you spend it? What part of the trip will you arrange in advance? How much will be spontaneous? Who will be responsible for the arrangements?

Dena Kaye also recommends that each of you should privately make a quirk list. The list consists of two parts. The first includes all the things that could happen on a trip that might drive you crazy, such as snoring, dawdling, or hogging the bathroom. The second part includes your own habits, needs, and preferences. Needs are different from preferences. Needs means such items as having to eat a full breakfast every morning, while preferences might include liking to sleep away from the window.

When you and your partner have finished writing your quirk lists, it's time to talk about what was written on each one. If you make your quirk list conscientiously and then

13

discuss what you wrote as honestly as possible, and you *still* think your partner and you can make a go of it, you have a good shot together.

No matter how well matched you are, your trip will be more successful if you set some rules before leaving. These may include:

- Planning how much time you will spend together, and agreeing to split up when one of you feels the need. You might say, "I'd like to see one more sight, and I know you've had enough. Would you like to shop (or hike, or swim) while I go? We could meet again at dinnertime."
- Agreeing not to push your partner into favoring your ideas. The trip won't really be ruined if your friend doesn't try escargots.

- Planning in detail how expenses will be shared each day. You should have a firm idea of how much you want to spend on each breakfast, lunch, and dinner, and how much each night's lodging will probably cost. Agreeing to discuss openly any big splurges or other possible exceptions to the plan will help.
- Agreeing beforehand whether or not you are open to bringing in more travel companions somewhere along the way, and if so, how that would be decided. Similarly, agreeing beforehand whether or not you are open to leaving one another in midtrip, and how that would be decided.
- Making use of each partner's strengths. Jim knows he's slow, so Mike is the trip's timekeeper, setting appropriate time spans for activities. "It's eight o'clock now. We'll meet at eight forty-five, after showering and dressing." The limits are set, and Jim has agreed to Mike's setting the timetable. Jim, on the other hand, is good at planning meals. He's in charge of shopping and cooking when the trip has slower moments. The meticulous care he gives to small details is appreciated.
- Agreeing on what belongs to each of you. Will you wear each other's clothing? Use each other's toothpaste? Comb? Borrow each other's money?

2. Getting There: Buying a Ticket

Use this chapter to find out how to travel when you need to buy a ticket—on an airplane, train, or bus.

Airplane Travel

Airplane trips usually provide the fastest travel between two points. When you travel by plane, you are usually given several choices for seating: first class, business, and coach are the usual terms.

Coach, being the least expensive, is the choice of most people traveling for pleasure. In coach, you are likely to sit three abreast. If you are in the air at mealtime, you will be given a two- or three-course meal. You may be offered several choices, and some may reflect the nationality of the airline. (For example, Scandinavian Airlines may offer *smørrebrød*, an open-faced sandwich served in Scandi-navian countries.) In coach, you have the attention of flight attendants. They provide magazines, decks of cards, or Band-Aids.

If you are seated in the first-class or business section, you will probably sit two abreast. Your seat will be roomier, though not by much. But it reclines farther, and it has a footrest. Your meal will be of higher quality, but again, not by much. The movie will probably be free, whereas it often costs about $3 extra in coach. You will also get more attention from the staff. It's true you might see a movie star in first class, but it's more likely that you'll sit next to a corporate executive buried in work.

First class is also lonely in contrast to coach. Coach bustles with excited travelers; seats in first class often re-main empty. Most important, the difference between coach and the higher-class seating is money. A first-class seat usually costs more than twice as much as one in coach. For example, a coach ticket between Minneapolis and Chicago costs $75. The same flight in first class will set you back $155. Between London and New York a coach seat may cost $696; in first class it may cost $1,998!

Fare Games

Buying an airline ticket is simple—you can buy one in person or over the telephone. It's deciding which one to buy that's not at all easy.

Do a lot of shopping beforehand. There are so many different fares offered for the same destinations that it's often hard to tell which carrier offers the lowest fares. Airline X may offer a low price but may make you travel at two in the morning. Airline Y can match the price, but has a three-hour stopover in Milwaukee. And Airline Z will give you the best deal, but wants full payment a month in advance and will let you stay only a week.

How can you choose among the many possibilities?

You can deal with the airline directly, work with a travel agent, or contact a computerized search service. Before you make a decision, though, you should look around on your own.

First, read newspaper ads to get an idea about general costs. Look for the fares of the older, established airlines. Compare them with the fares asked by some of the new, smaller companies, such as People Express, World Airlines, or Virgin Atlantic. If you use budget airlines, you can sometimes pay for your ticket right on the plane (as opposed to paying for it before the flight). On a budget flight you may get little or no food unless you pay extra for it, and you may not have a sheltered walkway to keep you out of the rain when you embark. What do you get in exchange? Savings of as much as 50 percent or more.

Whether you use the long-established airlines or the hot newcomers, fares change so frequently that travel agents can barely keep up. Computerized agencies such as Traveltron have sprung up. Their sole job is to track the best bargains, and you can now make reservations directly through them (see appendix). If you use these services to reserve a flight, the cost of their service is reimbursed. If you use the computerized search services merely for information, however, you must pay a fee of $5 or $10.

From time to time, the airlines go to war, dropping their fares dramatically to attract passengers. They may never again match the one-day offer Eastern Airlines made of a 29-cent fare between Boston and New York, but then, you won't have to line up for two days, as the customers did for that flight in 1981.

Once you buy a ticket, write the name of the airline, flight information, and any important numbers on a separate piece of paper. If you lose the ticket, contact the airline immediately. You will get a refund, but it sometimes takes months—you may have to buy a second ticket.

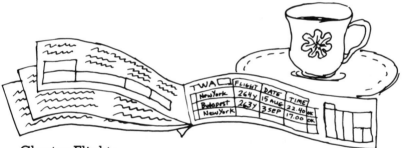

Charter Flights

If the airlines are not at war when you want to travel, you may want to investigate charter flights, another way to save on fares. A charter flight is really a reserved block of seats. If you buy a ticket for a charter flight, you are buying a seat for yourself on that flight and that flight only. Although the charter flight may be going on Delta, you do not have the right to shift to another Delta flight at another time.

19

Charter flights can offer wonderful bargains, but they must be examined carefully. Check the restrictions. Must you purchase a tour package to take advantage of the charter? How far ahead must you pay? If you cancel, can you get your money back? Are there additional taxes and service charges? Sometimes additional fees amount to about 15 percent extra. With the extra money added on, the charter may no longer be the great bargain it first appeared to be.

Charter flight prices depend upon when you travel. Before signing up, be aware that the low price advertised in a newspaper may only be available one or two weeks a year; all other weeks are more costly. Prices for charters are highest during peak travel seasons, such as Christmas, Easter, and the summer months.

Charter flights can run very smoothly, but they can also give you a large headache. You are buying a ticket for a particular flight. If it doesn't fill up, your entire trip may be canceled and it could be too late to book another inexpensive flight. Some charter flights are also known to have problems with departures. Flights may run on major airlines, or they may run on airlines you've never heard of. Ask your travel agent about your airline's record for on-time departures.

Even if a charter flight takes place on the day it is scheduled, if departure is delayed many hours, valuable time has been knocked off your precious vacation. If your return is delayed, you may be late for school or work, and you may inconvenience people who want to pick you up at the airport.

If you book a charter flight, use a travel agent with broad experience who can tell you about the record of the group and the airline you are signing up with. Whenever you book a charter, find out what the penalties are if you cancel. Again, since your ticket is only good for that one flight, it is usually harder to get a refund on a charter. Find out exactly what your rights are.

Other Options

Dizzy with choices already? There are still a few other ways to negotiate the air-travel maze. Occasionally, believe it or not, you'll save by buying a round-trip ticket even though you need to go only one way. This usually happens when a special round-trip deal is offered.

At other times you can save on one-way flights by getting a ticket to a farther point on a flight that has a stopover at your real destination. For example, if you need to go to Denver, but can purchase a flight to San Francisco with a stopover in Denver, it might actually cost you less to buy a ticket to San Francisco than one to Denver. You buy the ticket to San Francisco but get off in Denver. If you do this, make sure your luggage is properly marked so that it goes where you go.

21

Another way to save on airfares is to go standby. Some companies offer last-minute deals that lower the price substantially, but you must be packed, at the airport, and ready to leave, knowing full well that you can only get on the flight if the people who reserved earlier do not show up. If you are prepared to wait around as a few packed flights go off without you (or are even prepared to go home and try again the next day), this can be a cheap way to travel.

If you're lucky, you may even end up saving money by using overbooking to your advantage. In recent years, airlines have tended to "overbook" commercial flights, giving out more reservations than they have seats to offer. By doing so, they hope to make sure that each plane is filled even if some people don't show up for their reservations. When everyone does show up, some people must be "bumped." Imagine—you have waited all year for your trip to the Grand Canyon and you get to the airport but cannot get on the plane. You've been bumped and must wait for the next flight, or maybe the one after that. What about your hotel room in Arizona?

As you can well see, being bumped can make you furious. It can ruin a vacation. As public outrage has grown, the airlines have been forced to provide compensation to those who are bumped. Depending upon how many hours you are being delayed, if you are bumped, you may get a meal, free airfare, a free ticket to be used in the future (sometimes to the destination of your choice), or even cash.

If you're adventurous and have flexible plans on the

other side, you can volunteer to be bumped, hoping you will get another flight only a few hours later, perhaps with a super bargain or a free ticket in your pocket.

Remember: You can't plan on being bumped. Never pay for an airline ticket if you can't afford to use it.

More ways to save: You may want to join your airline's "frequent flier" club. Your travel agent or the airline itself can send you an application. Once you join, an account of the miles you log in the air will be kept in a computer. If you fly often, you accumulate bonus coupons for future flights—these range from better seats to coupons good for free tickets. Another bonus: You can get processed faster before your flight at a special check-in line for club members.

While the free tickets are most often merited by busi-

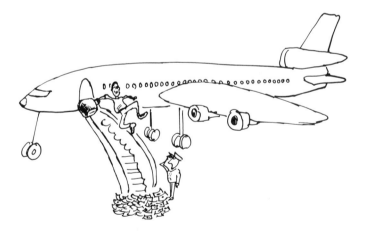

ness travelers who shuttle about in the course of their work, you can benefit from the clubs' coupons in another way. Many bonus coupons are legally bought and sold. Their sellers offer lower prices than the going rates. You can buy such coupons through newspaper ads or by going to a coupon broker. The process takes more than a month, so you must plan ahead. If you buy a coupon, make sure to ask about restrictions. Some airlines—among them Pan Am, United, and TWA—do not permit coupon transfers to people who are not related to the original purchaser, and you'd be taking a chance to buy one. Other restrictions may mean you cannot travel at certain times or on certain flights. Coupon brokers are listed in the appendix.

If you are over 18, you may be able to become a free-lance courier. This is another way to save on flights. Some businesses that send packages and baggage elsewhere may have no one to send along with the materials. A courier is hired through a courier agency to escort the baggage. If you can leave with little advance notice and you want to go where the agency has demand for packages, you may be able to save 50 percent or even all of your fare. Couriers can usually take only a carry-on bag because the checkable baggage space is taken up with the business materials. Couriers also have to be concerned about how they will get back home, for sometimes the assignment is only one way. Usually, though, the courier agency has frequent business going back and forth. Two courier agencies are Stratus Transportation Services and Archer Courier (see appendix).

Getting to and from the Airport

These days, airports are very crowded. Auto traffic jams going in and coming out are common. It can often take you longer to get to the airport, get processed for flights, and get away from the airport than it takes for the flight itself. This is truly a disadvantage of flying.

Give yourself plenty of time to get to the airport. Plan to arrive about an hour before your plane takes off. This will give you enough time to wait on lines, check your baggage, and go through any necessary inspections.

There are several ways to get to and from the airport. Find out how long each takes before making up your mind, and give yourself enough time so that you still have that hour at the airport itself. Here are some choices:

- A friend or relative can drive you and pick you up.
- You can hire a taxicab or limousine to take you anywhere you want. This can cost from $5 to $25, or more. If you choose to take a cab or limo, to avoid being cheated make sure you know what the distance really is and about how much it should cost. A travel agent knows or can find out. If you travel in a group, you should be charged as a group, not individually.
- You can participate in a prearranged group limousine service. In this setup you travel with strangers and will probably make several stops along the way. To get to the airport, you will be picked up either at

home or at a set embarkation point. From the airport, the car or van usually goes only downtown and/or to the popular hotels. You must make your own way from there. The cost per person is in most cases under $8, sometimes under $5. If you are traveling with several friends, it may pay to hire your own cab. At $5 a person, a group of four can afford a taxi for $20, and it will take them just where they want to go. For solo travel, the group limo arrangement is probably better.

You can use local city transportation. The ride on the airport bus or train is usually longer, but it can be a small tour in itself, visiting neighborhoods you otherwise would not have seen. Leaving the airport, the bus usually makes stops on its way downtown, and again, you are responsible for getting to your individual hotel. The savings are worth it—it costs only a few dollars per person, sometimes as little as 75 cents.

There may be even more than one type of local transportation available. An example: In the Port Authority terminal, the major bus station in New York City, signs advertise a nonstop bus to Newark Airport. The cost is about $4, and the bus is loaded with airport travelers.

However, there is also a commuter bus, which handles mostly local workers going to and from jobs. Its first stop happens to be Newark Airport. This bus costs about $2. It cannot accommodate large, heavy valises, but if you haven't any, you've saved 50 percent of the fare.

To find out about local travel arrangements, ask friends who've been there, a travel agent, airline personnel, and airport officials. If you are asking at an airport in a location new to you, make it clear which kind of transportation you are seeking.

Seating on the Plane

On most flights, seating is reserved before you board the plane. Many airlines will let you reserve your seat when you buy your ticket—you don't have to wait until you arrive at the airport. To get the seat you want, reserve as early as you can.

Most airlines offer smoking and nonsmoking seating sections, although on some shorter flights smoking is not allowed at all. When you reserve your seat, make sure to state all the preferences you have, including smoking or nonsmoking, window or aisle, and which side of the plane you want.

A hint: If, when you call the airline for reservations, you are told the seating you prefer is not available, take what they have but ask about both your flights again when you get to the airport to leave on your first flight. The airport personnel may be able to give you better seats on one or both flights. There are two reasons for this: Some good seats are saved specifically for distribution at the airport,

27

and there may be some last-minute cancellations. If nothing can be done as you are leaving, ask again at the airport on your way home.

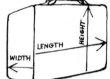

Luggage on a Plane Trip

When you travel by plane, your light luggage is kept on a shelf overhead or under the seats. For everyone's safety on the plane, this luggage should not weigh more than 30 pounds. Heavier, larger luggage is stored in the cargo hold of the plane and tagged at the time of check-in. At the end of the trip, you pick up your luggage on a conveyor belt or rotating carousel. Before you are allowed to leave the airport, you must present your matching luggage ticket to prove that the bags are yours.

When you are flying within the United States, you are allowed to bring three pieces of luggage. When you add length, width, and height together, one piece cannot come to more than 45 inches; the second cannot come to more than 55 inches; the third cannot add up to more than 62 inches. Each piece cannot exceed 70 pounds. It is likely you will take the 45-inch piece of luggage with you aboard the plane, but you can store it if you prefer.

When you are flying abroad, present international regulations permit two stored pieces (55 inches and 62 inches maximum) and one bag to carry aboard. Because of space limitations, this is likely to be in the 45-inch range. Once again, the 70-pound limit per stored bag applies.

Make sure that all your baggage is labeled (see chapter 8, on how to pack) and that anything you may need right away, anything breakable, anything that might react badly to being in a cold, unpressurized cargo hold (aerosols, lantern batteries, etc.), and anything irreplaceable is in your carry-on luggage. This includes your passport and IDs, traveler's checks, extra eyeglasses, drugs, prescriptions, and itinerary. Planes also tend to be cold—you may want to throw socks and a sweater into your carry-on bag.

All your baggage including purses will be inspected for weapons and explosives before a flight. This is done to prevent hijackings and other crimes. You will be asked to pass through a metal detector, and your carry-on bag will be put on a conveyor belt. It passes through an X-ray machine and a metal-detecting device. As it moves through the inspection machine, the inspectors can see a picture of some of the contents. Metal objects such as scissors show up.

To make sure you won't miss your plane, arrive early, with ample time for baggage check-in and security inspection. Sometimes there's a line at the machines. Occasionally hand searches are needed if machines are broken. Give yourself even more time if it's a busy travel season.

You can also help by being willing to open your bags and show your possessions. The law says inspectors can ask to see anything you're carrying. This includes the contents of your pockets. Wrap and pack things so you can repack quickly. While the inspectors have the right to hand-search anything they choose, you can also request for any reason of your own that your things be searched by hand instead of machine.

In the United States, most electronic security devices have low radiation. It is claimed that low-radiation devices will not hurt camera film. In other countries, the detection equipment is not low-radiation. Both here and abroad you may want to shield your film from X rays. X-ray exposure effects are cumulative. Each exposure adds to the chance that your film may be damaged. High-speed film should not go through the security device. Come to the airport with no film in your camera, in case you're asked to open the camera. You can place film in special bags camera stores sell, or you can ask the inspector to examine the film by hand. Allow extra time if you want to do this. It speeds things up if you have all your film in one place in your luggage, readily available for inspection.

Travel writer Paul Grimes says that security inspection is usually quick and easy, but it can become complicated if you aren't ready for it or if you don't take it seriously. Inspectors do not laugh at bomb or weapon jokes. Instead, they may hold you back for the most thorough check imaginable. You could miss your plane, and—believe it or not—you could end up in jail. Hinting that you have a gun constitutes giving false information. This is a federal offense and can result in a fine (up to $1,000) and/or going to prison (for up to one year). Obviously, there are better places to joke than at the inspection station.

Jet Lag

A lot has been said about jet lag, that discombobulation you experience after you've passed through different time zones quickly. You can help your body adjust in several ways.

The basic aim is to get to sleep at the time locals are going to sleep, even though it might be another time of day where you've just come from. Toward that aim, you will do better if you schedule your arrival for late afternoon or evening.

You can help yourself if you plan a stopover on flight sequences that last more than six hours. Whatever the length of your flight, eat lightly the day before you are to leave. On the day of departure, eat at the mealtimes of your destination. In *Overcoming Jet Lag*, authors Ehret and Scanlon recommend high-protein breakfast and lunch and a high-carbohydrate dinner. If you take a walk before bedtime, you will help your body relax.

If you must arrive at your destination in the morning, and you haven't slept much on the plane, you will help your body adjust if you don't rush out eagerly on that first day of vacation. It's hard to resist sightseeing, but reserving some rest time in the afternoon can save you days of fatigue.

Suggestions from Dr. John McCann, medical director at Pan American World Airways:
- Don't tire yourself by rushing to the airport or dragging heavy suitcases.
- Wear loose-fitting clothes.
- You may want to take your shoes off in flight.
- Move about the plane during the flight.
- Sleep as much as possible in the air.
- Drink lots of water to avoid dehydration in the rarefied air of jet aircraft.

Train Travel

Train travel is slow, but it can be relaxing. Train seats are comfortable. The individual cars are often uncrowded, and you can curl up in two seats. Unlike during car travel, you can exercise aboard a train. A walk to the dining car or snack bar can be a quarter of a mile, and there are plenty of fascinating people to observe along the way.

A train trip can become a social occasion. Many travelers are willing to converse on trains. And then there is the sightseeing, another advantage of train travel. The Rio

Grande Zephyr, for example, rides through the most breathtaking portions of the Rocky Mountains.

Amtrak (the National Railroad Passenger Corporation) is the principal United States carrier of passengers on the rails these days. Amtrak is sprucing up the system, modernizing stations, and offering tour packages to scenic areas of interest.

Tickets for train travel are available at many travel agencies, through toll-free telephone (1-800-USA-RAIL), or at the station itself. For most trips, you can buy either reserved or nonreserved seating, but sleeping-car arrangements are always reserved. An unreserved, standard-rate ticket is usually good for one year.

Generally, train travel is more expensive than bus travel but costs less than plane travel. There are exceptions, however, especially when you are traveling to destinations served by the low-cost airlines. Then, flying will probably be cheaper.

Amtrak makes discount travel offers. Some special fares require traveling during the weekend, when business travelers are not on the trains. Others require returning within a set period. Still others require staying within one region of the country; Amtrak has divided the United States into three regions—East, Midwest, and West. Right now, you can go from Seattle to El Paso and back for $150, because both cities are within the region designated West.

When you buy your ticket, remember to ask if the rate you are given is the lowest fare for your destination. Like the airlines, Amtrak has many different promotional offerings. For example, there are 14 different fares between Boston and New York!

Check to see if your ticket entitles you to a free stopover along the way—that is a valuable plus. Check also to see if Amtrak is the best bet for you. If you are not traveling long distances, you might save money by using local commuter trains instead of Amtrak.

Some Amtrak lines offer checked baggage service. When this is available, passengers may carry onto the coach only the baggage they will need en route (a maximum of two bags, except in sleeping cars). Passengers may check three pieces of luggage, weighing up to 150 pounds in all. No one suitcase can weigh more than 75 pounds, and boxes cannot weigh more than 50 pounds. Baggage must be labeled with name and address and checked a half hour before departure time.

Eurail Youthpass

If you are going to Europe, you may want to travel through the Continent by train. The Eurail Youthpass is available for travelers under age 26 (at a cheaper price than the adult Eurailpass) who live outside Europe or North Africa. The Eurail Youthpass card entitles you to unlimited second-class travel throughout 16 countries in Europe. These countries are Austria, Belgium, Denmark, Finland, France, West Germany, Greece, Ireland (Republic of), Italy, Luxembourg, Netherlands, Norway, Portugal, Spain, Sweden, and Switzerland. The pass also includes free or reduced-fare transfers for many steamships, ferries, and buses.

The Eurail Youthpass is convenient because European railroads stop throughout the Continent, in small villages as well as large cities. The trains run frequently and offer a chance to meet Europeans, see fine scenery, and relax without the strains of driving in new territory. Since the pass can be used as often as necessary, many travelers have used the trains as informal hotels, saving money by stretching out on the train seats.

Seating is not guaranteed on trains, but reservations can be made for a nominal fee. If you desire first-class travel, there is a first-class version of the more expensive Eurailpass, good for persons of all ages.

A Eurail Youthpass is a good travel buy if you intend to visit several countries and plan to cover more than 2,000 miles in a month or more than 4,000 miles in two months. The cost is presently about $300 ($290 in 1985) for one month and about $400 ($370 in 1985) for two months. One benefit of having the Eurailpass is the payment system. Since it is paid for before your trip, you don't have to fumble for the appropriate country's currency along the way.

You should buy your Eurail Youthpass in the United States; you may not be able to buy it in Europe. Passes are available from travel agents and at school travel bureaus.

Once a Eurail Youthpass is bought, you must begin to use it within six months of the date it is issued. When you board your first train, the pass is validated. From that date, you can use it until midnight on the last day it is valid. Therefore, if you buy a two-month pass and begin using it on July 1, you must finish your travels by midnight on August 31 to avoid paying extra.

If lost or stolen, the Eurail Youthpass can only be replaced if it has been validated and the validation slip is presented at a Eurail Aid office. Application for refund of an unvalidated (unused) pass must be made to the agency where the pass was sold.

If you travel through Europe, be aware that in crossing from one country to another, passports and other documents will be examined and occasionally luggage will be inspected.

A pass similar to the Eurail Youthpass is sold for travel in Great Britain, and foreign travelers visiting the United States have similar opportunities to buy low-cost passes for transportation here.

Bus Travel

Bus travel means different things to different people. For some, it is relaxing; for others, adventuresome. For still others, bus travel can be a test of endurance. You can't stop whenever you want, as you can in a car. You can't get up and walk around, as you can in a train. And you can't get where you're going fast, as you can in a plane. Buses not only travel more slowly, they may also make many stops along the route to your destination.

Why travel by bus, then? If you're traveling to a small city, bus travel may be the most convenient, most direct, and least expensive way to get there. In fact, it may be the only public transportation to that destination. Buses service many cities and towns that are bypassed by trains and planes. If you're traveling alone, going by bus may

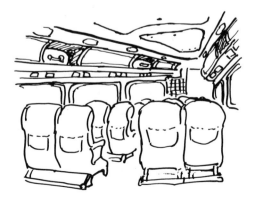

37

be cheaper than the cost of gas, tolls, and wear and tear on a car.

But surprisingly, many destinations are now more expensive to reach by bus than by plane. Nevertheless, some travelers still prefer the bus.

Bus travel allows you to see expansive landscape, or get a look at downtown city areas both in the daytime hours and at two in the morning—something you cannot do from a plane. Riding for seemingly endless hours may mean the opportunity to read a 300-page book, or the possibility of sharing secrets with a stranger you'll never see again.

Some bus riders even get a kick out of the grimy coffee shops in bus depots. Be aware, however, that while you can feel safe *on* the bus, you should be especially careful in bus depots. Bus stations are frequently in the seediest parts of town. Homeless people, drug addicts, and other questionable characters may find a comfortable place to rest in or near the depot. In some cities, young people harass travelers arriving at the terminals, demanding money to escort them to a taxicab. Hold your belongings close to you and do not go far from the depot on a stopover unless you are sure it is safe. If you are not at ease inside the terminal, stand close to the ticket booth, where the attendant can see you.

Getting Your Ticket

If the adventure of bus travel appeals to you, call the major bus companies to inquire about discounts for round-trip bus service, late-night traveling, and weekend excursions. Sometimes you can buy a pass for unlimited travel during a certain period of time. The typical passes are valid for 7, 15, or 30 days. You can crisscross the country several times if you sleep on the buses at night and do a lot of visiting and sightseeing in the day. However, if you don't intend to cover lots of mileage, the bus-pass plan may not be as economical as a plane ticket.

Other savings plans include a special fare for which you can travel one way over a limited time period (usually 15 days). Offers change from time to time, but right now you can travel between any two points in the system for about a hundred dollars. For coast-to-coast trips, this fee is better than plane fare, but if costs for food and lodging are taken into account, you may end up spending nearly as much for a less comfortable trip.

Bus companies make many special offers, so when you order your ticket, even if you are already given a discount, make sure to ask, "Is this the lowest fare?"

The major bus companies, Trailways and Greyhound, offer handicapped people the opportunity to take along a companion for free. Some local companies also extend the same courtesy. A doctor's note stating the reason a companion is necessary must be shown.

It is not publicized, but usually one company's bus travel pass will be honored on other carriers. Thus, you may be able to buy a Trailways pass and use it on Greyhound for part of your trip. The companies will extend this privilege to you if your company doesn't go to a particular destination. They will also let you switch if your company isn't sending out a bus for several hours and the other company has one leaving sooner. When you travel, carry bus route maps for both major carriers. They will help you plan for stopovers.

If you buy a pass, be sure to ask when it becomes valid. If it becomes valid the day you buy it, as the Trailways pass presently does, you may want to buy it at the last moment. That way, all the days the pass is valid will be spent on the road.

Some travel agents will handle longer bus trips, but most bus tickets and passes are bought right at the depot. Get to the depot at least one half hour before departure time, in case you have to wait on line to buy the ticket. The extra time will also help you get your choice of seat, since bus seats are unreserved.

Luggage on a Bus

There are several places for your belongings on a bus. A small package (lunch, a sweater) can go under your seat. A gym bag or other small carryon can be placed on a rack above the seats. If you are traveling in the summer and air-conditioning bothers you, make sure to bring a light jacket.

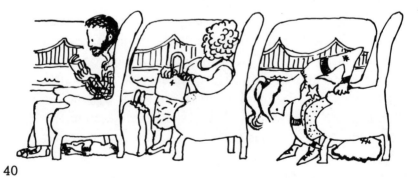

Medium-sized luggage is given to the bus driver, who slides it into a crawl space underneath the bus. You are allowed to store up to 100 pounds in the baggage area. The driver or ticket agent will probably give you a luggage tag for each piece stored in this area. You get half of the tag. The other half is usually attached to the suitcase. As a rule, your destination will be stated on the tag, so you can be assured the bag won't be dropped off in Boston instead of Portland.

Bus companies also sell boxes to ship disassembled bicycles and other packages. They can accommodate camp trunks, too. This larger luggage might not travel with you or on your bus, but it will get to the destination. The bus company can tell you how many hours or days it will take to arrive. You may have to bring large luggage to the station a few days early, and you may have to pay an additional fee. Nevertheless, if you're going to be in one place for an extended time, such as in camp or at a college, this might be the easiest way to ship your things. Always call the bus company ahead of time for such arrangements. Not all companies provide this service, and you may have to use another means to ship your belongings.

3. Getting There: No Ticket to Buy

This chapter tells about ways to get there without buying a ticket—in a car, on a bike, on foot, and hitching.

Car Travel

Car travel is convenient. You can take yourself right to the door at the time you want to be there, and you can comfortably carry most luggage and equipment. You can share costs with others, you can see the scenery, and you can stop along the way whenever you want. The freedom car travel offers can't be beaten, but to enjoy it you must also shoulder the responsibility of taking care of a car.

Some hints for a pleasurable car trip:
 · Before leaving, make sure the car is in good condi-

tion. Take the car to a garage for a checkup on the belts, hoses, radiator, transmission, and tires, including the spare tire. Have a lube and oil change. Make sure you have a way to pay for any unforeseen repairs along the way. If you're traveling with others, have a plan for daily and unexpected car expenses.

· Consider joining one of the auto clubs (see appendix). The clubs will give you maps and tour books, they will cash checks, and some will provide little extras, such as keeping a list of credit card numbers for you, but their most important service is getting you out of a jam. If your car breaks down, they help you get back on the road again. Membership is usually under $50 a year. Licensed drivers can join by looking up the local affiliate in the telephone book and calling for an application.

· Make sure the auto registration, insurance, and each driver's license will not expire while you are away. Take all necessary cards and papers with you on the trip, and don't forget an extra set of car keys.

· Get maps of your route from gas stations, motor clubs, and guidebooks. Plan your route in detail and study it so that you will be familiar with the highway numbers and can be a good navigator for the driver. Make sure your driving partners do the same.

· Plan for efficient packing. Will you need a rooftop carrier? If you plan to combine camping and motel stays, make sure you don't have to take out the tent every time you want just a toothbrush and underwear. Pack so that you know where everything is and can find whatever you need easily.

* Hide as many of your belongings as possible in the trunk or under a blanket. If your car doesn't look like a touring vehicle, it's less likely to be ripped off.
* Roll up windows and lock all doors whenever you leave the car.
* Check your oil, coolant, and tire pressure each day. Without enough oil, you can damage your engine. With inadequate coolant, your engine can overheat more easily. Over- or underinflation of tires causes excessive wear. Underinflation also lowers gas mileage.
* Follow prescribed speed limits and figure out how much driving you will do each day. Under ideal conditions, you can manage 100 miles in two hours. In mountainous terrain, you should plan on three or more hours for the same 100 miles.
* Stop driving *before* you get exhausted. If you're traveling with other drivers, you may want to switch drivers on a schedule. Every hour or a longer stretch of every 100 miles are good points for changing. When you make the switch, get out of the car and stretch your legs for a few minutes.
* Try to avoid traveling through cities or on city expressways at rush hours. This may necessitate leaving home or your motel at 6:00 or 7:00 A.M. and rearranging your normal breakfast hour; it may mean pulling into a motel earlier in the day than you'd normally want to, or it may mean stopping for a meal

somewhere until after the rush hour and getting into a motel rather late.

· Call home now and then. If you have borrowed a family car, you may have questions to ask, and your family will be more anxious to know you are safe than if you went by train or bus.

Getting Along in Traffic

Traffic and driving regulations differ from place to place. In California, for example, the moment a pedestrian steps off the pavement and into the street, a driver must stop immediately and give the pedestrian the right-of-way. In most places in the United States, a right turn on a red signal is permitted by law. However, certain localities— New York City is one—forbid it under most circumstances.

Even though you may be far from home, you are responsible for "doing as the Romans do." Otherwise you may end up with tickets and fines. If local authorities decide to, they can even put you in jail.

45

Driving styles can vary as much as rules and laws. A spin on a Los Angeles freeway can dizzy the most experienced driver; so can a bout with taxi drivers in New York City or Chicago. And many American tourists have been unnerved by European drivers who frequently inch up on the cars ahead of them, tailgating for long periods before passing.

It's possible to master driving in places that are foreign to you if you make up your mind to be more alert than usual. Whoever is driving must decide to give up looking at the sights to pay total attention to the road—and only the road—and concentrate on anticipating what might happen next.

Because driving in new or traffic-congested areas is so often tiring, it's a good idea to avoid extra driving in those places if you can. Metered parking is not plentiful in downtown city areas; on some streets parking is prohibited entirely. Finding free or inexpensive parking can take so long that you'll be sorry you went at all. Instead of driving everywhere, you may want to park your car at your hotel and ask the hotel clerk for directions on walking or taking public transportation to places you want to visit.

If you are planning to walk or to use local buses and trains, you may want to find a hotel downtown. Many cities have a number of clean, comfortable, and reasonably priced hotels right in the city center. Many of these hotels offer free or low-rate parking for guests. In Washington, D.C., for example, there are acceptable hotels within a five-minute walk from the Mall, where all the interesting museums of the Smithsonian Institution are. Even in the heart of winter you can get to the White House, the FBI, and other attractions without freezing or spending a dime for transportation.

Occasionally, certain hotels will help you avoid extra driving by providing bus service for guests. Many of the hotels near Disney World, for example, provide free or low-cost bus service to the park.

The management of Yosemite National Park has cut down on car traffic by installing free bus shuttles around the famous valley floor. You can be there for several days and use your car only on the way into and out of the valley.

If You Don't Own a Car

If you want to travel by car, but don't own a car, your best options are to team up with someone who does or to borrow a car from a parent. Other possibilities include rental, driveaways, and buying a cheap used car for use only on the trip. All these possibilities are not easy to arrange and present problems.

Most car rentals are not available to people under 21; in some states, the minimum age is 25. There are some exceptions: The minimum age may be lowered if you have a credit card, but this is an individual decision made by the car-rental agency. The minimum age may also be lowered to 18 for foreign travelers who show an international driver's license, a passport, and a return ticket. At any age, it's difficult to rent a car without a credit card.

If you are able to rent a car, look for a good deal.

Car-rental prices vary tremendously. Look for unlimited mileage deals. Check out smaller national companies and local agencies that are not members of national chains, and look into companies that rent used cars, such as Rent-a-Wreck and Ugly Duckling.

Driveaway and automobile transport companies allow you to decrease travel costs by driving someone else's car to a destination. The owner may be flying but will need his or her car upon arrival. Here, too, the minimum age is 21 or 25. You must travel directly, and within a pre-scribed period of time, but it is an inexpensive way to get somewhere.

Some daring travelers will buy a used car just for a trip, with plans to resell it afterward. If this will be your route, use the newspaper ads for best buys. Go for a car at least 5 years old but in good shape. Take the car to a mechanic for advice before buying it. The fee is well worth it, for the mechanic's expertise is in knowing if and when the car will require major repairs that make the purchase worth-while. Of course, even if the car gets a clean bill of health from the mechanic, you are always taking a chance on unexpected repairs en route.

Bicycle Trips

Travel by bicycle is an adventure worth considering. Once you've invested a couple of hundred dollars in a good ten-speed bike, it's inexpensive. There are no fuel costs, and you get to keep your means of transportation when the trip is finished.

A bike trip gives you exercise and allows you to appreciate every bit of the countryside along the way. Extensive bicycle trails in the United States and Canada make the experience more pleasurable. Long distances can be traveled on the TransAmerica Bicycle Trail (from Colorado to Canada). The Great River Bicycle Route runs along the Mississippi from its headwaters to Memphis. Other trails, such as the Oregon Loop Trail, follow coastlines. Some routes are set up within one national park (e.g., Acadia), while others go from park to park—you can ride from the Grand Tetons, through Yellowstone, and on to Glacier National Park on the Great Parks Bicycle Trail.

You must be in good shape to attempt a bicycle trip. Practice and buildup are necessary before your departure date. For several weeks, ride each day, slowly increasing the number of miles and difficult terrain you can handle.

A bicycle trip requires careful planning. You should know how many miles you're likely to go and where you'll stay at day's end. Distances for each day must be estimated fairly accurately, allowing extra time for hills and bad weather.

Before leaving, make sure you are able to fix everything on your bicycle yourself—and that no matter what goes wrong with the bike, you can repair it. Then you will be more secure.

Preparing equipment for a bike trip is tricky—you must carry rain and camping gear, tools for repairs, a lock, clothes, some food, and a helmet, yet you must keep the load light and balanced to ride well.

Bicycle shops, outdoor clubs, and other organizations can help you get started in cycling. Members will teach you how to repair a broken derailleur, where to get cycling gloves, and what to do when you get ''crotch rot'' (saddle sores).

The International Bicycle Touring Society and Bikecentennial provide maps, accessories, and information about routes and trips. The League of American Wheelmen provides a list of ''Hospitality Homes,'' names and addresses of people who accommodate bicyclists overnight. They also list ''Touring Information Directors,'' who are willing to help in planning bike tours. Perhaps best known is the American Youth Hostels, which sponsors inns and organized trips. A separate section on American Youth Hostels is found on pages 89–91, and the other organizations are listed in the appendix.

You can send a bike on a bus, train, or plane. It is usually sent dismantled and boxed. Bike boxes can be purchased from cycle shops, bus companies, Amtrak, or airlines. The bikes become insured personal luggage on the major bus lines. (The total weight cannot be more than 100 pounds.) On Amtrak, a bike can be one of your three pieces of baggage that may be sent to baggage-receiving stations. (Boxes usually cannot weigh more than 50 pounds each.) Airlines differ in their restrictions. Check individually on any fees you will be charged for shipping a bike.

Hiking

Hiking is probably the least expensive way to travel. It can be one of the most joyful, for you are accomplishing your goals purely on your own steam. To enjoy hiking, you must savor the slow pace of it. You trade speed for the chance to relish the deep purple of a roadside flower.

If hiking will be your primary means of transportation on your trip, invest in a good pair of hiking shoes with ankle support. Camping, outdoor, and sporting goods shops carry these shoes. Your pack and equipment should be of good quality, too, for you alone must comfortably carry everything you need—from first-aid kit to clothing.

Like a bicycle trip, a hiking trip requires careful planning and buildup. You will succeed if you take practice

hikes, walking longer each time, perhaps carrying more and trying harder hills. Make sure your shoes and pack are comfortably broken in before you set out on your big hike.

Before you leave on your hike, you will need to know how far you will travel each day, what you are likely to see along the way, and where you will sleep each night. Your planning should also include provision for your meals. Where will you buy food? How much food will you carry at a time? How will you cook? You will need a plan for emergencies, too. Some of the equipment and skills you need for hiking are the same as those you need for camping (see chapter 4).

Trail hikes can be planned with information from outdoor clubs. Most colleges and some high schools have outdoor or hiking clubs. They also may be in touch with regional organizations. These organizations provide maps and guides to places to stay. Among the famous associations are the Sierra Club, the Adirondack Mountain Club, and the Appalachian Mountain Club. Many of the clubs are active in maintaining the trails they tell you about, so they know their business backward and forward.

Another source for topographical maps and guides is the National Park Service. The Government Printing Office can provide prices. Bookstores sometimes stock government publications, and they also are sources for materials about parks and trails published by other presses. If hiking in the city is your pleasure, look in bookstores for walking guides to historic sites.

Hitchhiking

Hitchhiking is increasingly dangerous. You are smart to be wary about hitchhiking. According to *Where to Stay USA*, "it seems people are convinced that the potential for danger is greater for the hitchhiker than for the driver. In the past it was the driver who felt threatened."

Hitchhiking is not recommended. There are no federal laws against it, but most states prohibit hitching in the "roadway," or paved surface. While this implies permission to hitch on the shoulder, there is tremendous variation in police attitudes toward any hitching. Reaction can range from pretending you're not there to running you in.

Hitchhiking is not easy. Hitchhikers must be prepared to walk long distances. They must travel light and so are forced to leave behind things they'd rather have along on the trip. The posture of hitching is tiring: One hand must be free to signal to cars, while the other must balance a large sign, with the name of the place you're heading for written on it, that can be clearly read from afar.

Hitchhikers place themselves in serious jeopardy every time they hitch a ride. Hitchhikers have been mugged, robbed, beaten, raped, kidnaped, and murdered.

If you know this, and you still decide to hitchhike, be forewarned: Size up the occupants of the car you are entering. If the people seem tipsy or strange in any way, don't get in. If you see that you are outnumbered, look at the passengers carefully before getting in. You can decline a ride gracefully by pretending you merely wanted directions.

If it's too late—you've gotten into the car, but are getting funny vibrations and want to change your mind—try not to be shy. Ask to be let out. You might say you have to go to the bathroom. Also, try to memorize the license number of any car you hitch with.

When you're in a car, never interfere in the business of the occupants. If they want the windows down and you're a bit chilled, leave the windows down. You're their guest. If they're bickering, stay out of it entirely. If you're with them for an extended period, offer to pay a share of their gas and tolls.

Never hitchhike at night. The danger increases greatly. Drivers cannot see you—you could get hit by a car instead of getting picked up. In addition, you may give the wrong impression and become prey for drivers looking for trouble.

A woman should never hitchhike alone, day or night. A boy and girl together are probably the safest combination, and the most likely to get a ride.

If, in spite of repeated warnings, you attempt hitchhiking, increase your chances of survival by heeding the advice of the Travelers Aid Society of Detroit:

- Be visible, wear bright clothing, and stand where you can be seen.
- Carry as little as possible.
- Choose morning and late afternoon for soliciting long rides—lunchtime is almost impossible.
- Hitch on highways rather than expressways.
- Try to find people who are already traveling—people at rest stops and gas stations. It's better for you to pick your driver than for your driver to pick you.
- A little paranoia is fine.

4. Places to Stay

This chapter describes some common places you might stay on a trip—at someone's house, a motel, a guesthouse, a college campus, a Y, or a campsite.

Visiting

On many trips you're probably going to be a guest in someone's home. This can be great fun, but it can also be difficult.

In the plus column for visiting are:
* the money you save on hotels and meals
* the lively companionship you share with greater closeness
* the tours you get—guided by local experts, who

know where to go and will give you the inside story

There's a minus column, though:
* the room you may have to share
* the company manners you have to put on
* the real possibility that your friendship might get cooler instead of warmer with increased familiarity

Your visit will be most successful if you plan it in detail with your host beforehand, spelling out as many of the specifics as you can. This way everyone knows what to expect.

Before you arrive, try to find out:
* how to get there (traditionally, by the way, *you* are responsible for your transportation costs)
* how long you are expected to stay and about how much of your time will be spent with your host
* if your host's family knows about your expected visit
* where you will sleep
* the kind of activities you will take part in and what you have to bring (Will you be swimming, going to

a country club, camping with the family? Each requires different clothing and equipment.)
* any costs you might have
* any house rules or strong preferences
* how your host and you will recognize each other if
you haven't met before

Hosts appreciate your presence if you don't create inor-
dinate work, expense, or demands on their time. They are
usually still in the midst of their normal responsibilities and
can't put everything on hold to be with you. You will be
recalled affectionately if you think ahead, acknowledging
that they are going out of their way for you.

A token gift upon arrival is not necessary, but it is nice.
Some ideas: specialty foods, teas, or stationery (anything
that gets used up); a novelty, game, or puzzle for you and
the family to enjoy together. If you're comfortable about
it, an offer to treat for something during your stay is often
accepted (ice cream on a summer evening, for example).
Finally, a thank-you note after the trip is welcome. If you
write about the highlights of your stay, all the better.

During your visit, most hosts generally like it if you:
* are able to mesh fairly well with their waking and
sleeping times
* are happy with varied activities and can be just as
pleased by occupying yourself with a night of reading at home as with a tour of the town
* help clear the table and carry groceries in from the
car

- are willing to try their macaroni and cheese even though you're used to a different style
- ask when it's most convenient for your shower
- get out of the bathroom after 5–10 minutes, straightening it before you leave
- turn off lights when you leave a room
- ask before using the telephone and reverse charges or bill to your own home any long-distance calls
- ask before inviting guests of your own to someone else's house

Motels and Hotels

You may want to stay overnight in a motel or hotel. Think about your tastes and habits when picking a place to stay. Do you like to be in the midst of things—right downtown or along a busy highway? Or do you prefer quiet? Is dinner at 6:30 P.M. your last substantial food for the day, or are you the type who enjoys a midnight snack? If you get hungry before bedtime, pick a motel that has a late-night restaurant attached or one within a block's walking distance. If peace is very important and you can't sleep with noise, look for a motel off the main highway, so traffic sounds won't keep you up through the night.

In any area, the prices for a night's lodging at available hotels and motels can vary tremendously. The prices depend upon location and amenities. You'll pay more for a motel a block away from the San Diego Zoo than one a mile away. You'll pay more for a motel room that has a bathtub than one offering only a stall shower. Motel prices can vary by $10 or even $20 a night.

If you want to make reservations before leaving home, one way to do it is to call. The major chains provide free 800 telephone numbers. You can call 1-800-555-1212 for information and get the toll-free numbers of Holiday Inn, Sheraton, Best Western, and the other chains. Reservations for hotel rooms in other countries can be made by mail, by long-distance telephone, through a travel agent, and sometimes through the toll-free numbers of major motel chains. It's a good idea to reserve a room for the first night of your trip.

You'll want to ask of each chain: "I'd like a room for two in Grand Rapids, Michigan, on July 18. How much will it be?" The operator will quote a price and answer your questions. He or she should know how many beds the room has (an important piece of information), how to get to the motel from the highway, how far the motel is from tourist attractions, and what conveniences the motel features (Laundromat, restaurant, etc.).

When you speak to a motel chain operator, you needn't reserve a room right away. You can call several chains and find out all the facts before reserving. As crucial as price is, location is also important. One motel listed under Grand Rapids may be right off the major highway and will give you a good head start for the next morning's traveling. Another motel, also listed as being in Grand Rapids, can really be three to five miles west of where you'll need to be for the next day's travels. Since you will twice have to go several miles out of your way to stay there, you should weigh this time and gas mileage in your decision. Is it worth the trip if the motel is $2 less a night? If you make your calls with fairly detailed highway maps in front of you, you'll be able to see what the operator means by 2.4 miles southwest on Interstate 71.

Once you have decided upon a motel, ask about the terms of the reservation. Write down what you are told.

Be sure to ask:
 • Until what time will they hold the room?
 • What should you do if you know you'll be late?
 • What is the reservation confirmation number?
 • What is check-out time?

When you use the major chains that offer 800 numbers, you have quick dialing convenience, but you pay for it in higher rates. By using a major chain, however, you also know you'll probably be satisfied with the comfort and cleanliness of the room.

On the other hand if you want to save money, and are open to finding accommodations outside the major chains, consider the following.

61

- Around the country there are many lesser-known chains that specialize in economical lodging without frills. Some have installed 800 numbers in order to compete with the larger chains. These include Susse Chalet Inns, Econo Lodges, La Quinta Motor Inns, Red Roof Inns, and others. A list of inexpensive motel chains is included in the appendix.
- Some economy motel groups do not have 800 numbers but are excellent buys. An example is the Motel 6 chain. If you don't know if there is a branch of Motel 6 in Grand Rapids, there are several ways you can find out.

  The address of Motel 6 national headquarters is found in the appendix. A travel agent or reference librarian can also give it to you. Send for the nationwide brochure listing all the Motel 6 units. Another way is to call the information operator in Grand Rapids and ask for a phone number for Motel 6. A third way is to call a large city library that has phone books for many communities around the United States. The information service at the library will provide the number of a Motel 6 in Grand Rapids if there is one.
- Travel guidebooks and tourist council brochures often list smaller, family-run motels. Some don't have as many amenities but are still comfortable. Usually you must send a letter or make a long-distance call to reserve these rooms, and the proprietors may want a partial deposit or complete payment in advance.
- If you are the type of person who doesn't reserve in

No Star

advance, there is another way to save money on motel rooms. Drive off the major highways at check-in time. Look on your map for a parallel route that goes your way. You probably have to go only a mile or two to the left or right of the superhighway. In many cases, the road you will be seeking was the main highway in the 1950s and 1960s, before the interstate system was fully developed. This route is narrower and slower, but there the motels of an earlier era often remain. They are usually not part of the big-name chains, but are run by families. If you don't mind older beds, these can be good, inexpensive finds. The desk clerks may also give you a more personal reception, for they may also be the owners.

· Look for hotels instead of motels. Most cities—small and large—have a number of clean, respectable hotels that charge less than roadside motels. Many were

63

once elegant centers of activity. Although the men in top hats and women in gowns are long gone, these hotels can offer fascinating architecture and a glimpse into the past as well as lower prices. These hotels can also be a godsend when the motels are full.

Motel and Hotel Safety

When you arrive at your motel, you will be asked to show identification. Usually you are asked to pay in advance. Make sure you are getting the kind of room you want. You are entitled to see it before you pay.

Is it clean? Does the heating or air-conditioning work? Are the beds comfortable? Are there enough beds? If you are traveling with a friend and want to sleep separately, make sure the room has two beds.

As you settle into your hotel or motel room, be sure to check its safety. Does the door actually lock? How about the glass door leading to the patio or parking lot?

When you're in the room, double lock and chain all doors. Don't answer the door without asking who is there. When you leave the room—even to go to the main desk or down the hall—lock the door and take your key with you.

When you leave for the evening, wear or bring any expensive jewelry along or check it in the safety deposit box some hotels and motels provide. Better still, don't take gold, silver, and other valuable jewelry on your trip at all. If you want to wear jewelry, bring imitations you can afford to lose.

When you return to your motel, be alert. Have your keys ready so you are not fumbling in dark parking lots or hallways. Do not invite strangers to your room. If you think you hear someone inside your room, do not go in. Go to the front desk instead and inquire if maintenance people are in your room. The staff will help you find out just who is there and if all is safe in the room.

When you stay in a motel, check how you'd get out of your room if there were a fire. Where are the fire extinguishers, fire exit, and alarm on your motel floor? What is the quickest, safest way out of the building?

If there *is* a fire, remember these safety tips:
- If your room door is hot, don't open it.
- If the door is cool, open it cautiously, but shut it quickly if there is smoke, and stay in the room.
- If the door is cool and there is no smoke, you can probably get out of the room. Stay close to the ground, crawling under any smoke you find along the way.
- Never use elevators.
- If you stay in your room, turn off the air-conditioner.
- Fill the bathtub with water. Use it to wet all available sheets and towels. Stuff the wet linens around cracks in doors.
- Keep a wet cloth over your mouth and nose.
- Fill the trash basket with water and throw water on the hot walls.
- Try to stay calm.

Guesthouses and Inns

Travelers in Europe have long enjoyed staying in private homes and small guesthouses. Before the upsurge in motels, these accommodations (also called tourist homes) were abundant in the United States, too. They still dot the countryside and are available in cities as well. In fact, they are making a comeback. Some are now known as "bed and breakfast" inns, because of the breakfast that is part of the cost.

In guesthouses you do not get a standard motel room. What you get instead is usually a bedroom in someone's large house, often with the bath down the hall. The room might be plainly furnished, or it might be ornately decorated with a brass bed and oak antiques. Along with your room, you might get conversation with your host about architecture and local customs, a living room to share with other guests, or even a midnight snack or cooking lessons.

Prices vary widely in guesthouses, depending upon location and how much quaint atmosphere the hosts feel they offer. You can learn about guesthouses and bed-and-breakfast inns by writing to the chamber of commerce of your destination. Guidebooks are also available (see the appendix).

College Campus Stays

Many colleges make their dormitory facilities available to visitors whenever the beds are not occupied. Some offer beds year round, but most colleges welcome guests only during summer, winter, and spring vacation periods. That's when the regular students are away. Happily, these may be the very times you want to travel.

A vacation on a college campus is a lot of fun. You get a taste of life at that college; you are usually allowed to use the gym, tennis courts, pool, library, and cultural facilities. Often the college is host to a special group while you are there—you get the bonus of meeting these visitors. Taking up residence might be members of an international soccer team, a cheerleader school, or a music camp.

At some campuses you must take a course in order to stay. Here's your chance to get ahead in school, or to

study in an area that has fascinated you—bird-watching, sculpture, Egyptian history.

Many campuses are broader in their invitation, extending the welcome mat to "students, alumni, adults, families, and prospective matriculants." Nearly every reader fits into one of those categories. At many colleges, you can stay as long as you wish—overnight, for a few days, or for a few weeks.

At a college campus you sleep in a dormitory. Arrangements can vary from sharing a dorm room with strangers, with a bathroom down the hall, to having a private apartment. Meals (often all you can eat) can be included or you may be on your own for food. Prices for college room and board will almost always be lower than sleeping at a motel and eating in restaurants.

If a campus vacation interests you, look into the guidebooks listed in the appendix. You might use them to pick out schools that are close to sightseeing attractions. Examples: Hartwick College, in Oneonta, New York, is near the Cooperstown Baseball Hall of Fame; major league farm teams play baseball nearby. Montana State University in Bozeman is a good jumping-off point for visiting Yellowstone Park, the Grand Tetons, and Lewis and Clark National Forest. You can also use the guidebooks to pick out colleges abroad—how about the University of Oslo as a base for visiting Norway's fjord country?

The college itself may run sightseeing tours to nearby points of interest. Check with the student activities office to see if you are eligible. If you are, you won't need a car to visit Yellowstone, and you'll probably save some money, because college trips are often subsidized with college funds. As a bonus, you'll have the pleasure of meeting new people; they can become your friends for the rest of your college stay.

Guidebooks try to be comprehensive, but the writers can't always be aware of changes. If you want to visit or attend summer session at a college (anywhere in the world), and it is not listed in the guidebooks as welcoming visitors, don't assume that the school will not accommodate you. The college may have opened its doors or instituted a summer session since the guidebook was written. Write directly to the college.

Write two letters. Address the first letter to: Registrar, Summer Session, College, Location. Ask about summer session dates and offerings. Send the second letter to: Housing Department, Summer Session, College, Location. Ask about the range of housing during your target period. You may have a broader choice than living in a college dorm: Private residence halls and apartments, cooperative housing, or an international house frequented by foreign students may be available to you.

Whether you are visiting for a six-week summer session or planning to stay just three days, your campus vacation must usually be planned in advance. Most colleges require reservations. Because more people are catching on to this inexpensive, interesting way to have a good time, it's getting harder to reserve rooms. So if rodeos near the University of Wyoming or canoeing near the University of New Hampshire beckon you, send for information a couple of months in advance.

The Y and Other Community Centers

In many cities, the YMCA, YWCA, and other community agencies provide inexpensive lodging. The financial support of their sponsoring organizations enables them to offer inexpensive, safe, clean, and comfortable rooms. Accommodations vary from bunk beds in a dormitory arrangement to single and double rooms. Most often, the room will be furnished simply, and the bathroom will be down the hall. Usually the Y is convenient to downtown locations.

Local agencies set up their own rules. Some require stays of several nights or more, while others limit your stay to a night or two. Some agencies will house men and women together, while others segregate the sexes. Even if they are religiously affiliated, most accept guests from any denomination.

Rates range from $10 to $35 a night, and you are usually given access to the agency's fitness center, swimming pool, and restaurant. A few agencies offer group rates, tours of the area, and discount books to local attractions.

Because of their low cost, accommodations at community centers are very popular. If you plan to stay at one, it's best to work with a set itinerary and reserve your room at least two months in advance. Information about the national network of YMCAs and YWCAs is found in the appendix.

Camping

People of all ages enjoy camping. Camping may be backpacking in the woods, tenting on an island, or vacationing in a recreational vehicle.

Whatever your style, you will probably enjoy the national parks and forests. They offer spectacular beauty, spiritual inspiration, knowledgeable guides, and a great variety of natural attractions. Deserts and mountain ranges, oceans and glaciers, bare granite pinnacles and tropical rain forests—these and more are to be found in the national parks. Visiting the national parks and forests is a great buy. It costs a nominal fee to enter each park (from 50¢ to $3). For $10, you can purchase a Golden

Eagle passport, good for one year's admissions to all national parks, forests, seashores, and historic sites. The Golden Eagle pass is available right at the parks. Camping fees are usually additional, but these are modest and lower than in private campgrounds.

Visitors to the national parks can explore the areas themselves, or they can choose from a broad variety of daily activities: guided walks, historical lectures, mountain climbs, swimming, nighttime astronomy exploration, or demonstrations of "search and rescue" operations.

Each park provides hundreds of tent and recreational vehicle camping sites. In most cases, these cannot be reserved in advance and are distributed on a first-come, first-served basis. At the more popular parks, such as Yosemite, the Grand Canyon, and Yellowstone, campers line up in their cars at the gates very early in the morning to ensure themselves a place to sleep. Some parks also rent cabins and hotel rooms, and these usually can be reserved in advance. Most units in the park system include stores, showers, and laundries. Some offer restaurants and swimming pools; campers can be quite comfortable in the national parks.

The national forest system is not as "developed" as the park system. The areas are purposely left in a more natural state. Amenities are fewer but quite adequate. As a result, they tend to be less congested and attract campers who are more serious about their communion with nature.

Besides the national parks and forests, the United States has a fine network of state parks, too. These capitalize upon the unique natural features of each state (a seaside

campground along Chesapeake Bay, in Maryland, for example). Many state parks offer services similar to the national parks, such as ranger talks, campfire programs, and guided hikes.

Some of the most charming public campgrounds around are those run by local municipalities. Don't overlook these cozy county, village, or township sites. A source of pride to their administrators, these campgrounds will often surprise you with their scenic locations and amenities. Low in cost (sometimes free), these areas may unexpectedly treat you to flush toilets, showers, free firewood, and perhaps attendants who have time to share their knowledge of the area with you.

The government doesn't have a monopoly on camping. Private campgrounds abound. Some belong to chains, such as Kampgrounds of America, while others are independent.

Private campgrounds can be enjoyable. Their owners may be friendly and eager to please. For $12–15 a night (for two people), they may offer you the features of a resort vacation: swimming, game room, shuffleboard, or miniature golf. Horseback riding, fine dining, and entertainment may be available. At some private camp-grounds, you don't even have to bring a tent or recreational vehicle—you can rent a cabin.

On the negative side, however, you must remember that, without the uniform standards upheld by most government facilities, private campgrounds vary widely in quality. The campsites may be crowded one on top of the other, or there may be little shade. It's a good idea to check out your site for cleanliness and comfort before registering.

Information about camping areas is available in many guidebooks (see appendix). You can also write directly to a particular national park, the tourism department in any state, and the chamber of commerce for any area you want to visit.

Camping Hints

In camping, you get closer to nature. A popular camping motto is: LEAVE NO TRACE. Following it means protecting the wilderness and yourself. The aim is to leave the site as much like you found it as possible, so the next group will be able to enjoy it.

These ideas from American Youth Hostels will help you *leave no trace*:

- Don't leave food on a table or in your pack or tent. Animals that have lost their natural fear of humans will search for food, ruining tents and other equipment. Leave food in a car. If you are backpacking, the American Youth Hostels recommends stashing

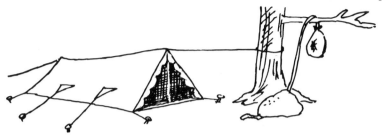

food in a stuff sack tied to a rope. Attach the other end of the rope to a small rock and throw it over a light tree limb that's at least 8 feet above the ground. You then hoist the sack toward the branch by pulling the end of the rope tied to the rock. The rope is secured to a tree or rock, leaving the food hanging a bit below the branch.

- Stay on marked trails at all times. If you create your own path, you damage the forest and put yourself in danger.
- Use an old fireplace at your site; don't make a new one. Fires should only be built on mineral dirt or bare rock, never where leaves, needles, or exposed roots are evident. Keep your fireplace contained with a circle of stones. Make sure water is available. Use dry wood from the floor of the forest for firewood. Never chop down branches of live trees.
- Keep your fire small, watch it carefully at all times, and allow it to go out completely by stirring the embers. Pour water on the ashes until the ground underneath is drenched. Feel any remaining charcoal to be sure it is cold, then scatter the ashes and place sod or dirt over the fireplace hole.

75

- Take any litter out with you. Don't bury it. Remove any aluminum or plastic that didn't burn in your fireplace and carry it out with you.
- Wash dishes and yourself away from natural water sources. Brushing teeth and shampooing in rivers and lakes, even with biodegradable soap, pollutes the water.

When using a tent for camping, bring the instructions for erecting it along with you and follow them carefully. Find as level a spot as you can for putting up the tent.

American Youth Hostels offers these reminders on tent camping:

- Remove from the tent site all rocks and twigs big enough to puncture the tent or cause you discomfort.
- Take off your shoes before entering the tent. Don't light matches or candles in tents.
- Air out wet tents at the first opportune moment. Your nose will tell you why when you unroll one that's been wet for a while.

Here is a basic checklist of supplies you may want for camping:

- tent and ground cloth
- eating utensils
- deep plate (preferably metal, for cooking)
- collapsible unbreakable cup
- plastic scouring pad

- insect repellent
- sweat shirt, sweater, or wool long-sleeved shirt
- cotton long-sleeved shirt
- rain gear (jacket with hood, and pants)
- nylon jacket
- hat
- towel
- biodegradable soap and dish
- first-aid kit
- sewing kit
- day pack
- flashlight and extra batteries
- lantern (rechargeable battery, unleaded gas, etc.)
- suntan lotion
- canteen
- sleeping bag and mattress or pad
- pocketknife
- compass
- matches in waterproof container
- toilet paper in plastic bag
- 20–30-ft. nylon cord
- extra plastic bags

5. Try These Vacations

Here are some vacation ideas you may want to try. Information follows about resorts, theme parks, package plans, teen tours, youth hostels, the Council on International Educational Exchange, and boating vacations.

Resort Vacations

Resort vacations are very popular because they offer so many activities. You can usually find almost any sport you desire at a major hotel, lodge, or dude ranch. Most meals are sumptuous, and you needn't search around for swimming, tennis, exercise classes, and evening entertainment—everything is available right on the premises. There may even be too much to choose from, and you might have to miss miniature golf if you want to play bingo. Friends with different interests can travel together but go their separate ways during parts of action-packed days and evenings.

Elaine Grossinger Etess, former co-owner of the famous Grossinger's Hotel and Country Club, suggests that to enjoy a resort vacation more fully, you should not be afraid to ask questions from the first moment you make contact with the hotel staff. The reservationist knows if you can rent a tennis racquet, if men must wear jackets to dinner, and when the swimming pool is open. When you get there, you should read the hotel directory placed in your room. Resorts are large—the layout can be confusing. Where is the area for horseback riding? What's the quickest way to the dining room? Read the directory, and if you still can't figure it out, ask.

At a resort, the cost of your stay is determined in part by the type of room you select. You pay more for a private bath, a larger bed, and indoor access to the main house. The fancier the room, the higher the cost. Mrs. Etess points out that if you choose a simple room, you still get an excellent bed, plus the same food and activities as someone who might be paying almost twice as much. You also pay less if you share the room. Since little time is spent in the room, these are good ways to save money.

School and youth groups frequently schedule weekends at resorts. If you go with an organization, you will probably pay less than if you make the reservation on your own. It's a good deal—groups are given sizable discounts. Equally important, nearly all your costs—including tax and tips—will probably be calculated in ad-

79

vance and you can pay it all in a lump sum. There may even be a few lessons and rental of sports equipment thrown in for free. If you go to a resort without group sponsorship, you will probably pay for each aspect of the vacation separately.

Resort reservations can be made by telephone or through the mail. Be aware that the individual rate you are quoted for a resort vacation does not include all the costs. Full participation in a resort vacation may mean spending up to one-third more than the quoted rate.

Tax will be added. There are extra fees for sports equipment rental (skis, skates, even Ping-Pong balls), tennis court time, and any lessons you might want. Generally, you pay the bills for your room, equipment, and lessons at the end of your stay, but your obligations are not finished.

You are also expected to tip the waiter or waitress and the person who cleans the room. If you use the services of bellmen and room service, you will be expected to tip them, too.

In the directory at your bedside in a hotel there is likely to be a guide to tipping. Each fee is computed by examining union contracts and average tips over a period of time. You are not bound by the guide's recommendations but can tip more or less, as you desire.

Bellmen, bartenders, and room service staff are tipped each time you use their services. The person who cleans your room is tipped at the end of a weekend stay. If you are assigned one dining room table for the duration of a weekend, then dining room staff are tipped when you leave. If you are not given a permanent table and can shift around (called round-robin seating), you should tip after each meal.

If you are staying at a resort for longer than a weekend, it is recommended that you give part of your tip in the middle of the vacation. Also, if you have special needs, it's a good idea to give part of your tip on the first day. Then you're more likely to get fast service if you ask for extra towels or want lettuce and tomatoes when they're not on the menu.

A recent tipping guide at the Concord, called the world's largest resort, gives these figures:

* Bellman $1.50 per person on your check-in and check-out
* Waiter/waitress $4.00 per person per day (three meals)
* Busboy $2.00 per person per day (three meals)
* Chambermaids $1.75 per person per day
* Room service $1.00 per person for breakfast and lunch
  $1.25 per person for dinner
* Bar waiters and bartenders   15 percent of your beverage check

Theme Park Vacations

If you visit a large amusement or theme park, you can get more pleasure for your money if you prepare. Cheryl Slavinsky, the public relations manager for Hershey Entertainment and Resort Company, suggests that you do the following before you arrive at a park:

- Write to the park in advance for rates, opening and closing hours, nearby attractions, and sleeping facilities.
- Check the brochures for special opportunities to save money. These include: off-season rates; two-day admission plans; preview plans that allow you to enter in the evening and return the next day; sunset plans, which allow reduced admission if you come only for an evening.
- Look for promotional coupons to reduce costs. They can save you about one quarter of your admission charge or give you more for your dollar in the park. Coupons can be found in local and national newspapers, and on food products ranging from milk containers to hot-dog packages. Sometimes the best offers are found right near the park—at gas stations, fast-food restaurants, convenience stores, and motels.
- Consider camping. Hotels near the major parks tend to be expensive.

When you get to the park, you will have a better time if you:

- Get a map and a schedule when you come in. Use them to plan which shows you want to see and to choose a meeting place if you should get separated from your friends.
- Avoid crowds by arriving early. If you go straight to the most popular rides or go as far away from the entrance as you can, you will have a shorter wait than at midday.
- Eat your meals a little earlier or a little later than the normal hour to avoid the crush. You may want to eat lightly so that your stomach isn't upset on the rides.
- Take a break in the middle of the day. Slow down at a show, avoid the heat in an indoor restaurant, or leave the crowded park entirely to go for a swim.
- Return from your break when you're rested. Remember that the crowds thin out during the evening hours and you can get onto the most popular rides again.
- Don't forget to wear comfortable walking shoes and bring any necessary clothing along—a sweater for the evening, a poncho in parks that tend to have a lot of rain.

Package Plans

If you are going to Hawaii, London, or just about any-place with a tourist trade, you may be interested in a package plan. It works this way: Tour operators fashion a trip for large groups of people going to the same desti-nation. Because they are buying space for many people, tour operators can obtain good discounts from hotel and charter companies. They often offer lower prices than you might get if you reserved plane tickets and hotel rooms on your own. And besides getting a good price, you don't have to do all the work yourself.

Package tours vary widely in what they include. Some offer only a flight and hotel room. You are on your own for meals and entertainment. Some packages go to the other extreme, planning for every moment—a welcoming party, side trips, all meals, even a farewell banquet. There are also package plans that take a middle road, planning some activities but also allowing you some free time. When choosing, it's important to think about how much you want to do on your own and how much you want to be in the company of others.

Compare several brochures for packages to the same location. Make no assumptions about what is included and ask about anything that is not explained in the brochure. A package is only valuable if you will actually make use of what is included. If meals are included but you will be eating at relatives' houses, you might want a tour that costs less and does not include food.

Check these features when you evaluate a tour:
* what time of day and day of the week you will depart and return
* if there is a choice of hotels
* how many nights in a hotel are paid for
* how many meals are provided
* if you can choose among several restaurants (a policy called dine on the town) or must go everywhere with your group
* if you can choose your meals from a menu or if they are set beforehand
* if any special dietary needs will be accommodated
* the facilities in the room and at the hotel
* how far the hotel is from the main tourist attractions you'll want to visit
* the number and likely age group of people on the tour
* if local bus tours are included
* how you will be escorted (the tour may be unescorted, fully escorted by one director, escorted only by local guides whom you meet as the tour moves, or managed by a director with help from local guides)
* if transfers from and to the airport are paid for

- if airport entry and exit taxes are paid for
- if any insurance is paid for (health, loss of baggage, cancellation of the tour)
- if tips are provided for
- if there are any extras included, such as a rental car, theater tickets, amusement park admissions, or sight-seeing tours
- if there are refunds for whatever you will not be using, such as meals
- how much free time there will be

In most cases you will be booking a package tour through a travel agent. Always read the pages in the tour book that indicate terms and conditions, especially those paragraphs in small print.

Whether you want a package that includes only the flight and hotel, such as many of those that are offered by International Weekends, or an all-inclusive luxury package, like those of Maupintour, you will do better financially if you are flexible about the day and time you leave.

If you are free to sign up at the last minute, you can get an even better package deal. The source is a travelers' clearinghouse. Clearinghouses work this way: If a plane leaves with empty seats or if a hotel has unbooked rooms, the money those seats and rooms would have generated is lost. Tour operators call a clearinghouse a few days or a week before departure and allow the clearinghouse to offer the unsold spaces at discounts of 20 to 50 percent.

An example of such a service is Moments Notice. After paying a membership fee, you and your entire family can take advantage of offers throughout the year. Information is in the appendix.

Teen Tours

If you want to travel with people your age but don't want to plan everything from scratch, you may want to sign up for a teen tour. There are many to choose from. Today, you can travel in the style you enjoy. You can tour close to home or trek halfway across the world. You can camp, hike, or bike. You can visit with families, stay on college campuses, or sleep at luxury hotels. Your trip can be a tour of the most popular tourist attractions, or it might be a highly specialized exploration, such as an archaeological dig.

Look for announcements of teen tours from Ys and civic agencies. Other sponsors include religious groups, universities, high schools, scientific and arts organizations, and private camps. Check with the American Camping Association and your school's counseling/guidance staff for ideas.

It's also a good idea to talk with people who've already gone on the tour you have in mind. If the director is not willing to give you names and phone numbers of past participants, you should regard that as a bad sign about the quality of the trip.

The criteria for selecting a teen tour are similar to those for all package tours, but in addition, make sure you know:

* how many participants are expected (10–30 usually work out well)
* the age range of the participants
* how many of the participants are boys and how many are girls
* how many leaders will be on the tour (at least 1 for every 10 participants is desirable)
* how old the leaders are, what their experience with teen travel tours is, and what is expected of them on the tour
* what is expected of you in terms of group living
* how much spending money is needed for meals and snacks
* how you can reach home and how you can be reached
* how you will be cared for if you are sick or hurt
* group policies regarding smoking, alcoholic beverages, drugs, and sexual activity

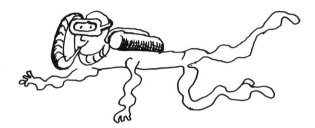

Youth Hostel Vacations

Around the world, hostel vacations promise active, energetic outdoor recreation. Some Ys and other organizations schedule hostel trips, but most are offered by a network of youth hostel associations. In the United States, the primary group is the American Youth Hostels (AYH).

AYH can mean time spent biking, hiking, canoeing, skiing, or even scuba diving. With AYH as your sponsor, you can learn backpacking skills, bicycle repair, or sailing. You can experience group living in hostel dormitories all over the world. Eventually you can be trained as a leader, to pass on your outdoor skills to others. AYH also offers other services: equipment sales and rental, charter flights, Eurailpasses, and International Student Identity Cards.

An AYH trip can take you a few miles from home or as far away as China. You can stay away a day, a week, a month, or a school semester. You can plan your own trip and use the hostels as overnight places to stay, or join an already scheduled trip mapped out by AYH. Organized trips vary in difficulty, and AYH offers guidance in selecting a trip that's appropriate for your skills and background.

Whether you use hostel facilities on an independent trip or join a tour, you must be a member of the hostel organization in your own country. Membership costs between $10 and $20. With membership, you have access to hostel travel and activities in 61 countries. (See the AYH address in the appendix.)

Your membership entitles you to sleep in the youth hostels. Directories to these communal homes are available through the hostel offices. Hostels vary from converted schoolhouses to fishermen's inns. Hostelers usually sleep in dormitory rooms, with fees of about $5 a night.

Hostels are not cheaper hotels. Rather, they are living models of a philosophy that stresses cooperation and environmental awareness. Each hosteler pitches in with cooking and light cleanup. You can arrive at a hostel by bike, on foot, or by car, but to preserve the spirit of simplicity and enjoyment of the outdoors, hostelers are usually asked not to use cars during their stay.

Each hostel provides bunks, mattresses, blankets, and pillows, but you need to bring the hostel regulation sleeping sack. It can be bought or made. (See instructions in the appendix.) Some hostels will rent sheets to you. Most often, sanitary regulations prohibit use of sleeping bags.

If you choose an organized bike trip run by AYH or a similar agency, you will have the company of young people your age who are eager to exert themselves in an adventurous encounter with the natural setting. On an AYH trip, participants meet local people, learn self-sufficiency, grapple with problems of group living, and become more self-confident.

An organized AYH trip will have one or two leaders. (Bicycle trips of 7–10 participants that last fewer than 18 days have one leader; longer trips and those with about 12 participants have two. Backpacking trips have 6–8 participants and one leader.)

Leaders are given lengthy training. They learn what they then teach participants: map reading, route planning, cooking, camping skills, environmental and nature study, hostel customs and rules, and above all, safety procedures, including first aid and rules of the road.

Before an AYH trip, if it's possible, participants get a chance to meet the leader. If not, they always receive a call or letter from the leader before the trip begins.

Participants receive detailed instructions on equipment selection and maintenance and are advised of any preliminary training that's needed. They are informed of AYH rules: Hitchhiking and use of drugs (including marijuana) are not allowed on any trips worldwide, and alcoholic beverages are not permitted on any North American teen trip. Group members on teen trips may not participate in intimate sexual activity.

During an AYH trip, participants, leaders, and parents are supported by a 24-hour telephone hotline. The hotline is used for contact in emergency situations. It's also used when leaders and group members cannot resolve disagreements or group living problems that arise en route. At those times, a fresh perspective from an outsider can be very valuable.

International Education

A number of organizations sponsor educational exchange programs. Probably best known is the Council on International Educational Exchange. This group cooperates in sponsoring over 800 exchange, study, and work programs throughout the world. You can be involved for a couple of weeks, a summer, a semester, or an entire year. Through its agencies, you might spend a working vacation as a hotel clerk in Ireland, a sheepshearer in New Zealand, or a grape harvester in France. As a volunteer in an international work camp, you might work with young people from all over the globe in renovating a civic center in Switzerland, building a hiking path in Czechoslovakia, or working with nursery school children in Germany.

The Council can enroll you in a broad variety of study programs, from fashion design in London to photography in Tangier. The projects may range from living with a family and studying language in Cologne to re-creating an Iron Age village in Denmark. The Council can also link your school up with a partner school in Japan, Venezuela, or other countries to exchange students and faculty.

If you don't wish to participate in one of the Council's formal programs, it can still be of service to you as a travel agency for students and youth. You can buy and carry the Council's identification card, which is widely recognized and accepted for discounts on travel and admissions. You can use its low-cost transportation, accommodations, insurance, and tours as a way to meet people and save money at the same time.

Among other organizations sponsoring campus stays, study tours, and stays with foreign families are the following: the American Institute for Foreign Study, Experiment in International Living, and Putney Student Travel. (See the appendix for addresses.)

Boating Vacations

You might enjoy a boating trip. You can book a boating trip for overnight, a few days, a week or two, or even longer. You can use a ship as a means to cross the ocean to Europe, steam down the Mississippi, sail around the Gulf of Mexico, cruise among the Hawaiian islands, or canoe along the banks of the Kennebec River in Maine. You can even sign up for a boat trip that doesn't stop at any ports. These "cruises to nowhere" give passengers a chance to enjoy being on water and away from land for a while.

If you want a vacation on water but aren't interested in the entertainment or seven-course meals offered on a luxury cruise, there are other alternatives. One is a windjammer sailing trip (see appendix) in the Caribbean, Maine, and elsewhere. It is less formal, less expensive, and more exciting. A windjammer cruise may be casually luxurious or may require passenger participation in the running of the vessel.

Another alternative is passage on a freighter. Some cargo ships take paying passengers along on their route. Usually you have food similar to the crew's; there is little or no entertainment. The itinerary is only roughly set; you have to be prepared to arrive in a port a day early, a day late, or possibly not at all. A freighter trip is much less predictable than a cruise or a windjammer trip.

Freighter travel is best suited for a particular kind of person, one who has a flexible schedule. He or she has an appetite for adventure and mingling with workers en route, but can also find joy in long hours alone. (See the appendix for information about freighters.)

Boating trips are not limited to these choices. Organized trips are also available on barges, canoes, houseboats, steamships, rafts, and other vessels. Travel agents and outdoor clubs are good sources of information.

6. Finding Out

This section of *Taking Off* is a potpourri of resources. Once you know where you might like to go, you will want to find out about your destination. The information will help you plan and enjoy your trip.

Suppose you want to go to Disney World and Epcot Center. You might want to know: Are there campgrounds near Epcot? Where can you go dancing at night? How old do you have to be to rent a car in Florida? How much does a day at Disney World cost? What kind of coat do you bring to Orlando in January? With enough information, you can get a clear picture of what your trip will be like, including its cost.

There are many ways to find out about your destination and what it offers.

Tourist Bureaus

Tourist bureaus and organizations are happy to supply you with advertising brochures, maps, and other booklets. Foreign countries maintain tourist organizations in the United States. Their aim is to provide information—everything from restaurant listings and shopping guides to walking tours. Most of the information is free because they hope to entice you to go and see their country for yourself. The tourist bureaus for other countries are usually located in New York, but branches may exist in other major cities, such as Los Angeles, Boston, Chicago, and Houston. You can get the address by calling your public library information service.

If it's information within the United States you want, tourism is promoted by chambers of commerce, convention and visitors' bureaus, and travel councils at most locations. The chamber of commerce is a board of business people in town. A convention bureau or travel council is a coordinating organization whose members are the owners of restaurants, motels, and attractions that provide tourist services. Their aim is to get more people to visit and enjoy their area. Together the members publish brochures and guides to their area. You can look in a phone book for your destination or contact your public library information service to find out which organization sponsors your destination.

Whether you are going abroad or staying in North America, make sure to ask for what you want specifically, so that the tourist council can send you the best brochures for your needs. If you are going to Philadelphia, and you want names of inexpensive hotels near Independence Hall, say so. If it's annual festivals that interest you, indicate that. Likewise for brochures about walking tours or some of Philadelphia's more than 100 museums.

Motor Clubs

Motor clubs are another source of information. The American Automobile Association (AAA) is the best known, but Exxon, Amoco, Texaco, and others offer services for travelers. They publish guidebooks to tourist attractions, hotel and restaurant listings, and maps. Some of the clubs will provide materials even if you are not a member. A list of organizations you can send to for information and membership applications is in the appendix.

Airlines

Many airlines provide free and inexpensive information. Most of their brochures are guides to major cities and tourist areas, but some airline companies have prepared booklets on packing techniques and how to travel alone. Call individual airlines for a list of their offerings.

Travel Guidebooks

Travel books can help you plan your itinerary and make selections among hotels, restaurants, and tourist attractions. Most bookstores and libraries stock an up-to-date collection. Some books are guides to general geographic areas, such as the *Mobil Guides*. Some aim to save you money, such as Frommer's "On $X a Day" books or "Fodor's Budget" books. Some, like the "Let's Go" guides, are geared to students' needs. Other guidebooks appeal to special interests, from backpacking and canoeing to finding bed-and-breakfast stopovers. Also available are pocket guides, dictionaries, and phrase manuals to help you find your way in a foreign language. Many guidebooks are listed in the appendix.

Word of Mouth

Friends and relatives are among the best sources of information. People who have visited your destination have stories to share. Take advantage of their willingness to tell you about their trip and to show slides. It's the people who've been there who let you know about the free county campground that provides complimentary firewood, or the restaurant on the second floor of the racquetball club that features comedians on Tuesday night.

Reading Material

Once you know where you're going, read as much about the area as you can. As early as possible, try to get maps. Without them you cannot get an accurate idea of how far you can safely and comfortably travel in one day. Maps also give the locations of campgrounds, state parks, colleges, and tourist spots. You can get maps from many of the sources mentioned above, and an occasional local gas station will still oblige.

The telephone directory for your destination is your complete guide to hotels, movies, auto rental agencies, churches, doctors—anything that concerns you. Using the directory, you can get a firm idea of the size of a city and the scope of its facilities. You can call and speak directly with local merchants, order things in advance, and set the stage for your visit. You can look at out-of-town phone books in a large public library or, for a few dollars, your local phone company will send a directory to your home from any area in the United States. Call the telephone business office to make arrangements.

Local newspapers from the area you'll be visiting can

give you additional information. The ads tell you where local people eat and where they might go on Saturday night. You can also find coupons that are redeemable at local stores. Large cities often have one newsstand that sells out-of-town papers. Public libraries may stock the newspapers of other metropolitan areas. If you cannot get a paper in advance, buy one shortly after you arrive.

Don't overlook the value of fiction in giving you a sense of an area, its history, and its people. A well-written novel conveys the feelings and images of having been there.

Travel Agents

Travel agents can help you plan almost your entire trip. They can arrange for flights, rail excursions, package tours, bus trips, and hotel stays. Travel agents do some of your legwork, and the service is free. Their efforts are paid for by the airlines, trains, and resort companies with whom they arrange your trip.

Costs for travel fluctuate continually and can become complicated to figure out. There are often seasonal

changes, and fares to popular destinations are altered frequently. With the help of computers, travel agents keep track of the changes and available discounts.

You can walk into any travel agency and ask to talk about your trip. Good travel agents will take time to sit down and discuss your ideas. They will try to find out what you'd really enjoy. They can map out the various ways to go and show you the comparative costs. They can figure out whether it pays to take a package deal or if you'd be better off booking a flight but planning everything else separately. They know how to find their way through the maze of possibilities to put together something pretty close to your needs.

Travel agents can also give you advice based on their own experiences. They have usually done a lot of traveling themselves and may know, for instance, that one West Indies island offers mostly beaches, while another has exciting nightclubs.

If you want to be certain that your travel agent is experienced and ethical, make sure the agency is accredited by either the American Society of Travel Agents,

Inc. (ASTA) or the Association of Retail Travel Agents (ARTA). Both organizations protect customers from being cheated. Look for an ASTA or ARTA shield on stationery, entrance doors, and store windows.

When you visit a travel agent, have a basic trip outline in mind. Know how long you can be away, how much you have to spend, and the activities you'd like. Try to find newspaper ads for vacations that sound appealing and feasible. If the agent seems knowledgeable and helpful when you present your ideas, you will probably make a good team.

Look for an agent who
* is friendly and listens
* is familiar with the kind of trip you're considering or who knows how to find out
* goes out of the way to discuss your choices, or who offers suggestions for saving money on your trip
* tells you both the strengths and weaknesses of a particular vacation plan
* is candid about terms used in the vacation brochures (Does "bustling" mean busy with excitement, or overcrowded? Does "rustic" mean charming, or run-down?)
* answers all your questions
* makes everything clear—how and when you'll go; how and when you'll pay; what you'll get; if specifics such as tips and insurance are included
* writes the plans down in language you can understand

Most travelers want to get going at the same time. We yearn for warm Mexico and the Caribbean in January and cool Cape Cod and Puget Sound in August. Holidays during which people are off from work and school are always popular times to vacation. Because the demand is highest at these times (called peak seasons) prices are, too. Of course, in peak seasons you may also get crowds.

You may gladly pay peak-season rates if it's the only time you can get away or the only time you can take the kind of vacation you want. After all, you can't do much skiing in Utah in July. But if you *can* be choosy about your vacation time, you can usually cut expenses by traveling when other tourists aren't banging the hotel doors down. Off-season visits often present opportunities to meet local people. In September or May the man in the post office has time to show you a shortcut to the coast; the hotel manager may tell you the history of the Indian trail you just hiked. Before you travel off-season, however, make sure that the activities you like can really be enjoyed when you will be there. September or May are fine for lighthouse exploration and trail hiking, but less satisfactory for swimming. Also, some facilities (local museums amusement parks, restaurants, shops, etc.) may be closed during off-season.

Local Sightseeing Tours

If you are visiting a city that is new to you, and your travel package does not include a bus tour, you may want to sign up for one. A guided tour gives you an immediate feeling for the area, an overall view of how it's laid out, and glimpses of highlights you may want to see on your own later. The bus will probably pass notable museums, monuments, parks, and stores. It may loop through ethnic enclaves that merit a return visit.

You can select a tour of Denver or Zurich and sign up for it with your travel agent. Word-of-mouth advice about which tour to take is usually reliable, but if you haven't heard about any particular tour, the travel agent or the tourist offices of foreign nations and domestic cities will give you a list of names.

If you don't want to book a day trip in advance, you can wait until you get there. A hotel concierge will book it for you, or in most cases you can simply walk up to the departure point an hour before the tour is scheduled. Some people prefer this method because they can go when the weather is good and their mood is right.

7. Practical Matters

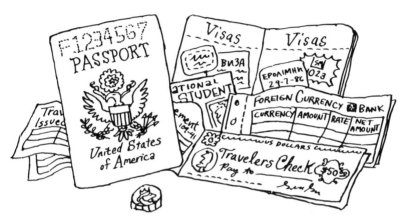

This chapter is about the practical things you must handle before you set off. It includes information about identification and passports, money matters, and correspondence.

Identification

Whether you travel to the next city or the next continent, you will need to carry identification. You will be expected to be able to prove who you are on many occasions. Proof may be requested when you register for a motel room, leave a deposit for a tour, or rent a car. If you should be stopped by police or other authorities, you will also be required to show identification.

You can identify yourself with a driver's license, a school identification card, or an officially registered International Student Identity Card. If you leave the United States for Canada or Mexico you will also need proof of citizenship, and, of course, if you go abroad you must have a passport.

The International Student Identity Card is a worthwhile purchase, especially for travel abroad (the cost is about $10). With an International Student Identity Card, you often qualify for discounts at hotels, plays, museums, and other attractions. You become eligible for many student tours. You can obtain the card at many university travel offices and the Council on International Educational Exchange, AYH, or Harvard Student Agencies (addresses in the appendix). You are eligible for a card if you are a full-time student or have graduated within the past year. To apply, you must show up-to-date proof of your student status. This could be a transcript, dated ID card, or signed letter from the registrar with an official school seal. You must present a small photo (vending-machine type), with your name printed on the back, and proof of your nationality and date of birth.

Passports and Visas

To apply for a passport, look in the white pages of your telephone book under United States Government. There should be a State Department subhead, with a Passport Agency subsubhead under that. You can also call your local post office to ask who handles passports in your town.

John P. Caulfield, a press officer with the State Department's Bureau of Consular Affairs, says: "Typically, people look into their holiday options, decide on their destination and then apply for a passport. The process should be reversed. People should get their passports first, since with a passport in hand they can go virtually anywhere."

A passport is valid for 10 years if you are 18 or over, 5 years if you are 17 or younger. March through September are the busy months in passport-processing offices. If you apply during the rest of the year, your papers will be processed faster. If you are planning a summer trip, get a comfortable head start by beginning the passport application process by March.

To obtain a new passport, you must get together the following:

- a passport application—you can get one at a passport office, post office, and from some travel agents
- a certified copy of your birth certificate if you were born in the United States, or a consular report of your birth or naturalization papers if you were born abroad
- proof of identity—driver's license, banking card, student identification card, etc.
- two identical photos 2" × 2" in size (vending-machine types are not acceptable in this case)—often a passport photograph studio is located near the passport office in larger cities
- money for the passport fee—the processing fee is about $42 for those age 18 and above and approxi-

mately $30 for those under 18 for new passports, $35 for all renewals.

When you have collected all the above, you must apply in person to start the processing machinery. Depending on where you live, you could be bringing your materials to a passport agency, a federal or state court, a post office, or the office of a county clerk.

If your passport has expired within the past 8 years, it can be replaced without your having to go through the entire passport procedure described above. Call the agency handling passports in your area and find out if you are eligible. If you are, get an "Application for Passport by Mail." This application can be obtained at passport agencies, post offices, and some travel agencies. You must complete the form, and attach your old passport and two current identical 2" × 2" photos. The photos must be signed on the back. The package must then be mailed to the local processing agency.

If you will be traveling in foreign countries, you may need visas and vaccinations, and you may want to have an international driver's license if you are eligible.

A visa is a stamp on your passport that gives you permission to travel in a foreign country for a certain amount of time. You can find out from a travel agent or the foreign consulate or embassy of the country you plan to visit whether you need a visa. The consulate or embassy will provide a list of documentation needed for the visa application; a travel agent should have the forms.

Because of the presence of diseases such as yellow

fever, cholera, and malaria in certain countries, you may need vaccination. It's your responsibility to tell your doctor exactly where you're going, and since many doctors don't have occasion to give vaccinations frequently, it's good to know what you need before you get to the doctor's office. Vaccination information is available from your local health department or the foreign consulate or embassy. You can also send for a free brochure, *Health Information for International Travelers*, c/o Superintendent of Documents, United States Government Printing Office, Washington, D.C. 20402.

Make sure to arrange for your shots several weeks before you leave. Some vaccines must be specially ordered; others must be administered in more than one dose. Planning ahead also gives you time to recover from any sensitivity reactions.

International driver's licenses are available from regional offices of the American Automobile Association or from the American Automobile Touring Alliance (see appendix). An international license is good for one year. To apply, you need a valid American license and two passport-size photos (vending-machine type will do). The cost is under $10.

Money Matters

Your money is safest if you bring traveler's checks on the trip instead of cash. If the checks are lost or stolen, the agency that issued them will replace them for you within a short time. Personal checks cannot be relied upon because they usually cannot be cashed out of your home state. You should start your trip with some cash—no more than you would need for two days—and use traveler's checks all along, keeping at most a two- or three-day cash supply in your wallet.

You can get traveler's checks at most banks and some service agencies. You may be charged 1 or 1.5 percent commission, but a bank may supply them at discount or free if you keep an account there. Commission-free checks are also available if you shop around. American Express traveler's checks, for which you are usually charged a commission, are issued free by AAA to its members. Other free checks include Thomas Cook and Deak-Perera.

American Express traveler's checks are probably the most widely known and easiest to cash. American Express also offers traveler's services if your checks are lost or stolen. Besides replacing the checks, it will cancel credit cards and help you get temporary identification. In your emergency it will send a single mailgram or international cable for you. American Express travel service offices will also cash personal checks up to $200, and they will arrange alterations in your motel, airline, and rental car reservations.

The procedure for buying traveler's checks varies among the issuing agencies. Some banks will accept a personal check for the entire amount. Others will accept a check only for small amounts, such as $250, and want the rest in cash if you don't have an account with them. Check by telephone before carrying large amounts of cash through the streets.

How much money in traveler's checks should you have? Figure out how much money you will actually need on your trip, subtracting the cost of anything that has been paid for in advance, such as airline tickets. Include money for lodging, food, entertainment, souvenirs, and travel from place to place. When you have your figure, add about 10 percent.

It's a good idea to overestimate the amount of money you will need. That way, you won't be caught short. The checks can always be redeemed at the end of the trip.

When you know how much you need, bring your cash and/or check payment to the issuing agency. An officer will help you convert the dollars to traveler's checks in various denominations. Ask for checks in low denominations (mostly $10s and $20s, perhaps one or two $50s), so that you can cash them easily in restaurants and local stores.

You will be asked to sign each check once in the issuing agency. There is also a line for you to sign once more on each check. The second signature goes on at the time you cash the check—that's how you prove the checks are yours. On a trip you must remember *not* to put that second signature on until the store or restaurant has agreed to take the check. The cashier should *see* you sign.

Find out how to replace your checks if there is trouble. Most issuing firms have 800 telephone numbers to call. You must also make plans for record keeping. Each check has a serial number. Write the serial numbers down on a list. Make two copies and leave one home with your family. Keep your list *separate* from the checks, so that if the checks are lost you will have the list with the numbers to report to the issuing agency.

Check the serial numbers on your traveler's checks from time to time. Some sophisticated thieves steal every fourth or fifth check, thinking it won't be discovered for days.

If you have credit cards, make sure you have the identification numbers and expiration dates on a list. As you do with the traveler's check serial numbers, keep the list in a separate place, so that if the cards are lost or stolen you can quickly call, cancel the cards, and limit your liability.

If you are not eligible for a credit card in your own name, sometimes you can be issued a card in your parents' name. Or you might be able to make an arrangement with your parents to carry the number and expiration date of one credit card on your trip. If you work out the details in advance, you can use the number to purchase plane tickets over the telephone.

You should safeguard your money and valuables at all times. Unfortunately, tourist areas also attract thieves. Some are even children. Lock your car wherever you go. Don't leave your pack on a bus terminal bench while you get up to read an advertisement.

Beware of pickpockets, especially on crowded streets, public transportation, and in parks and department stores. If you wrap a thick rubber band around your wallet, it won't slip out of your pocket as easily.

Many travelers buy money pouches to wear on belts or around the neck. (You can get one in a good camping store.) If you carry money in a wallet, keep it out of sight. A front pants pocket is safer than a back pocket. A pocketbook should have a zipper. The zipper should be kept closed at all times. The moment you remove a pencil from the bag, zip it closed, even though you will be putting the pencil back in almost immediately. Get into the habit of zipping the bag anytime you remove or put in something. The bag should be held close to your body—not swinging—and you must be especially careful with shoulder bags, since the straps can easily be grabbed or cut.

You may want to invest in a carrying case for your most important pieces of paper and plastic: licenses, credit cards, duplicate list of traveler's checks, identification cards, etc. If you keep the carrying case separate from your wallet and cash, and your money is stolen, at least you won't lose your important credentials, too. It's difficult enough to replace cards when you're home. It can be a nightmare on the road.

You cannot carry a duplicate of your passport. If you lose it, go immediately to the U.S. embassy and the staff there will help you replace it. The procedure can take several days, because the information must be verified with the State Department in the United States.

A reminder: Before you leave on your trip, remove any unnecessary cards from your wallet or carrying case. You cannot use a Kansas City library card in San Mateo, so why risk losing it?

It's wise to be prepared. Read the information about what to do if you run out of money (chapter 9). With planning and a little luck, you will never have to use it.

Money Exchange

When you are in another country, you will make most of your purchases with the local currency—lire in Italy, pounds in England, and so on. Many stores will accept only native currency; others charge extra to take American dollars. You will need to exchange dollars for the proper currency.

Say you are planning a two-week trip: one week in England, then a second week in Italy. Before leaving the United States, figure out how much currency you'll need for your stay in each country. Remember to subtract any lodging or other expenses that have already been paid for. Then find out if there are any monetary restrictions. Some countries limit the amount of United States currency you can bring in and the amount of local currency you can take out. Travel agents and the consulates of the countries you'll be visiting—in this case, England and Italy—can give you the information.

Now make a plan. Find out the central bank exchange rates from a newspaper, library, bank, or travel agency. There may be last-minute fluctuations in the pound and lira, but you'll have a general idea.

Before leaving the United States, you may want to get enough pounds for the beginning of your stay in England. Have enough so that you can buy food, use the telephone, or pay for a taxi. You can always get more in England, but make sure you have enough to tide you over for a couple of days. You may want to get enough lire for your first couple of days in Italy, too, or you might plan to get that amount just before you leave England.

Each time you need more British currency in England, exchange American money only for the amount you expect to use. As you get ready to leave England, try to use up your pounds and pence as much as you can, so that you are not left with them in Italy.

When it's time to move on to Italy, make sure you have enough lire to get started there, and when it's time to return to the United States, make sure you have American dollars and coins with you.

You can make money exchanges in banks, airports, hotels, and major stores. Usually, you get a better rate if you make the exchange in the country itself, exchanging dollars for lire in Italy and for pounds in England. Exchange rates vary. Shop around a bit before exchanging large sums. See where the commission is the smallest. You are likely to get more foreign currency for your dollar when you present traveler's checks instead of cash, because traveler's checks move faster through the banking system.

Or you can follow this advice. R. Leslie Deak, of Deak-Perera U.S. Incorporated, always recommended taking the following on your trip abroad: 25–50 percent of what you expect to spend in U.S. dollars—mostly in traveler's checks; 50–75 percent in foreign currency—mostly in traveler's checks denominated in foreign currency.

Customs Inspection

When you return to the United States and when you travel between other countries, you must make oral and/or written declaration concerning the items you have with you. You will be asked what you bought abroad. If you bring in more than the monetary limits set by the Customs Service, you must pay a duty (tax) on the excess amount.

You can be searched at the customs desk. This is more likely to happen if you are returning from a so-called

high-risk country—one that has a lot of narcotics traffic—
or if you are not cooperative with the customs inspectors.

You will ease your way through customs inspection if
you do the following:
- Register items manufactured abroad with the customs inspector before you leave the United States.
  Have serial numbers ready. Show the customs inspector your prescriptions, also, to prove that they
  are not narcotics.
- Declare openly what you have bought, including
  any new clothing you're wearing, gifts, etc.
- Become knowledgeable about items purchased
  abroad that are duty-free. Learn which purchases are
  not allowed to be brought into this country (fireworks,
  pornographic materials, switchblades, items made
  from skin or feathers of endangered species, certain
  meats, fruits, etc.). You can get information from your
  travel agent and the government. Write for a free
  booklet, *Know Before You Go: Customs Hints for
  Returning United States Residents and Trademark
  Information for Travelers*, United States Customs Service, Department of the Treasury, Washington, D.C.
  20229.

Staying in Touch

There are numerous ways to keep in touch with friends and family while you are away, from letter writing to using tape recorders and computers. You may want to ask people to save your correspondence. It makes an excellent journal of your trip.

If you plan to use the phone to keep in touch, you might arrange to call home at a specified hour when your family can be there to receive your call. It should be a time when they are usually home and when the rates are low. Many travelers choose a weekend hour. If you use this method, once the time is set, it's your obligation to call as close to the hour you've set as possible to avoid needlessly worrying those awaiting your call. If you have changed time zones, that must be taken into account so the call is received at the right time.

If you are not staying in one place on your trip, such as a college campus, but are moving about instead, you can arrange to receive mail and calls by mapping out an itinerary for your family and friends. "Around the tenth of August, I'll get to Arnold's in Tucson. I'll stay there two or three days. Here's his address and phone number."

People can also write to you anywhere in the United States by using the post office's General Delivery system. Tell everyone the approximate dates you will reach certain points. Letters must be addressed very carefully, reading: Your name, c/o General Delivery, name of town, and the zip code of that post office. The zip code will ensure arrival at the right post office. That's especially important in larger towns and cities. Use a zip code directory or telephone book to determine the right zip code for the area you want. Each envelope should be labeled "Please Hold for Arrival." It will be saved for two to four weeks, after which it is returned to the sender. If you want mail from General Delivery, you will have to identify yourself to prove the letters are yours.

In most foreign countries you can receive mail addressed to you c/o Poste Restante at the main post office of the town you are visiting. Be sure to tell your friends to highlight your last name—write it in capital letters, or underline it—since in some countries the family name is written first.

American Express runs a travel service throughout the United States and in major foreign cities for those who have its credit card or traveler's checks. Letters addressed c/o American Express will be held for a month. You can get a directory of travel service offices at any American Express branch.

8. Packing

No matter how many trips you take, it's very hard to pare packing down to absolute essentials. The more you travel, the better you get, but something is inevitably forgotten and a couple of unnecessary items are unavoidably dragged around. This chapter will help you keep the forgotten and extra items down to a minimum.

The kind of trip you are planning determines your choice of luggage and what to put into it. Consider the following:
  • *Your method of traveling.*
      If you are using a car with lots of trunk space, you can take much more—sports equipment, a pillow, your hair dryer, and a summer's supply of stationery. If you're flying, you have to pick and choose more

carefully. The baggage you choose depends upon the size and shape of whatever you'll be carrying.

· *The weather.*

Weather is your first consideration in deciding if you need bathing suits, sweaters, and boots. Using travel guides, newspapers, and the advice of friends, you can find out the weather in any part of the world for any time of year. Make sure you get the average temperatures for both day and evening, as they can vary in some locations by 30 degrees or more.

· *Plans for your time.*

If there's nothing you'd like better than to loll on the beach all day and dance at night, then you may want to include more bathing suits and brightly patterned shirts or blouses than would someone who is off to tennis camp. The tennis camper will probably make room for more than one tennis racket and will leave out the flowered shirts.

· *Length of your trip.*

The amount and variety of what you must take depend in part on how long you'll be away and how you plan to launder your clothes on the trip. If your trip lasts between three or four days and a week, you have a choice. You can decide to pack a heavier load, and include a variety of clothing and underwear for each day. Or you can pack less and wash clothing by hand once or twice. If your trip lasts more than a week, you may get tired of seeing yourself in the same clothing if you don't pack a variety.

No matter how long your trip is, and no matter where

you are going or how, it is wise to follow one simple rule when packing: You should be able to carry what you've packed. Remember, the root word in luggage is "lug." Since you will be carrying your bags through airports, to motel rooms, and up and down stairs everywhere you go, make sure you can manage your luggage without help. One way to test this is to take a short hike carrying your packed luggage. Try walking a few blocks with your suitcases or backpack. If you get tired, it's a signal to leave more at home.

Several weeks before your trip, make a list of everything you'll need. By making the list with plenty of time to spare, you can add to it as you think things through. "Oh, yes, insect repellent . . ." A list also gives you the opportunity to delete items.

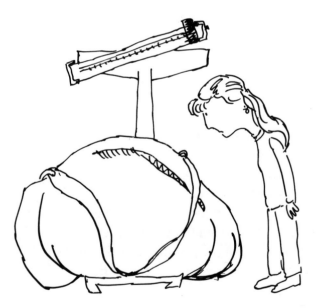

The next step: After you've mulled over your list for a week or more, find a place to set aside your belongings for the trip. Lay your things out on a bed, couch, or table. Arrange your possessions in categories. Place all cosmetic items together, all socks together, all underpants together. This way you can count them and avoid duplication.

Give yourself several days, preferably a week or more, to look over what's been set out. This will help you make sure almost nothing important is left out but extras are cut. Experienced packers stress the discipline of bringing along only half of what they originally had in mind.

Choosing Materials and Clothing

Everything you pack should be the smallest of its kind, of the lightest weight possible, unbreakable, and easy to care for. Small amounts of shampoo can be poured from large glass bottles into sample-sized plastic bottles; the same goes for vitamins. Toothpaste can be purchased in the smallest tube available.

Most of what you take should be already used and comfortable for you. Clothing should be laundered at least once by the method you will be using on the trip, to make sure it doesn't wrinkle. Walking shoes should be broken in a couple of weeks before the trip to make sure they are suitable for the rigors of travel.

Clothing for travel should pack and wash well. Blue jeans, T-shirts, and most wraparound skirts are good choices. Permanent-press, stain-resistant fabrics that can be washed by hand and drip-dried are best. Loose-fitting clothing is comfortable for walking and sitting in cars and buses.

As much as possible, each piece of clothing should go well with the others. Keep the number of colors small. It helps if you limit yourself to two or three shirts or blouses and two or three pants and/or skirts, including what you intend to wear on the first day. Remember that dark colors will hide stains and small wrinkles better. Try to keep accessories to a minimum, too, bearing in mind you can pick up almost anything that becomes necessary along the way.

A Traveler's List

Here is a sample packing checklist for a one-week summer trip. As you can see, it is too long for light packing. It is meant as a working list of ideas. Each trip is individual; a week of camping requires different preparation and equipment from a week spent at a luxury resort.

- two pairs of pants
- two pairs of shorts for warm weather
- two or three shirts, blouses, and/or T-shirts
- three pairs of underpants
- two pairs of shoes
- one sweater
- one blazer, jacket, or trench coat
- three pairs of socks and/or panty hose
- two bras
- one skirt

- one scarf
- one hat
- sleepwear
- bathing suit
- towel and washcloth
- brush and comb
- toothbrush and paste
- deodorant
- soap and soap dish
- razor
- sanitary napkins or tampons
- toilet paper
- any necessary medications (including vitamins)
- prescriptions for any medications
- extra eyeglasses/contact lens equipment
- prescription for eyeglasses/contact lenses
- insect repellent
- auto registration
- driver's license

- car insurance form
- extra car keys
- traveler's checks and cash
- travel tickets and receipts for reservations
- money pouch
- credit cards or personal checks
- proof of citizenship/ID
- passport
- first-aid kit: Band-Aids, adhesive tape, gauze ban-dages, absorbent cotton, antiseptic, ointments for burns, aspirin

- small sewing kit and safety pins
- string, rubber bands, rope
- maps and guidebooks
- pen
- small notebook/address book
- scissors
- tweezers
- cosmetics
- travel iron
- hair dryer
- shampoo
- cold-water soap
- premoistened towelettes
- plastic bags (for packing wet clothing or separating clean clothing from laundry)
- jewelry
- travel mirror
- nail polish
- calamine lotion
- suntan lotion
- hot-water coil
- packets of instant coffee, soup
- pocketknife
- can opener
- pillow
- air mattress or sleeping pad
- flashlight
- canteen
- matches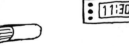
- alarm clock

- day pack
- rain gear
- collapsible umbrella
- deck of cards
- tennis racket or other sports equipment
- camera
- extra camera batteries
- film
- radio
- binoculars
- a memento from home

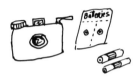

(Note: Unless your electrical appliances are equipped with adaptors for the different currents and plug shapes of other countries, don't include them when you're packing for a trip out of North America.)

Luggage

Once you have a tentative idea of what you will need on your trip and how you will be traveling, you will know what kind of luggage you need. The choices today are numerous, from backpacks through vinyl suitcases to hanging garment bags. Luggage gets a lot of use and abuse. It gets thrown about in airports and scuffed on graveled walks. In general, the more you pay for your luggage, the better its quality will be and the longer it will last.

Hikers, hitchhikers, and bus riders usually prefer backpacks. Backpacks leave one's hands free to count change or open a map. It is important to try on any backpack you are considering for purchase. Fill the pack with items that will be as heavy as the gear you plan to carry. (You can actually bring your gear in a box into the camping store or weigh it at home. Good outfitters may also have weights to approximate your load.) When the pack is filled, put it on, ask to have the straps adjusted, and walk around the store. If the straps are comfortable and the balance feels right, the pack might be a good one for you.

A pack that takes the beating of travel will cost at least $75. For backpacking, a pack with an aluminum frame is preferable because it transfers the weight from your shoulders to your hips. An exterior frame can accommodate more weight, but an interior frame has no outer metal to catch on poles. If your pack is merely serving as a substitute suitcase, however, an interior frame or frameless backpack is easier to throw on buses, trains, and airplanes.

Look for packs that have pockets for small items so you

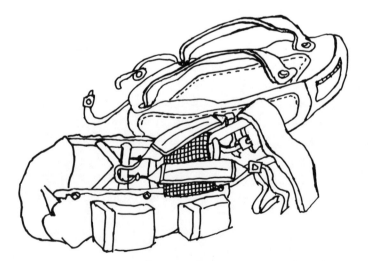

can reach for a knife or address book easily. A front-loading pack is also easier to work with than one that loads from the top. More is visible, and you won't have to dig for your underwear. "Let's Go," a series of travel guides written by Harvard students, recommends packing heavy items up the inside wall of the pack. If you don't, you will be pulled backward and could have back problems after walking many miles with the pack. Depending upon the shape of the pack, however, some hikers find that loading heavy items at the bottom is best.

If you choose suitcases over a backpack, you might want to carry two bags. One in each hand will lend body balance for walking and each can be lighter than one heavy bag would be.

Today's soft-sided luggage is attractive for its light weight and expandability. Small- and medium-sized canvas, nylon, and vinyl bags stretch to accommodate an astounding amount, giving a greater capacity than the older rigid materials. Look for bags that will fit in the small areas under airline seats and on bus shelves. Call the airline or bus company for exact dimensions if you need them.

Walk around the store carrying the cases you have chosen. If possible, load them. See how the handles or straps feel. If they feel comfortable and do not make red marks on your palms or shoulders, the bags may be appropriate. Other features to look for in bags include outside slots, brass zippers, adjustable straps, zippered compartments inside and out, and studded feet on the bottom.

If you need more formal clothing than jeans and simple skirts on your trip, you may opt for a hanging garment bag with a metal frame. Its hangers can hold dresses, pants, and suits, and there is less chance of wrinkling. Many garment bags have zippered sections to store shoes and other accessories. The garment bag can be hung in a motel closet, so you won't have to unpack. When you are traveling, the garment bag folds in half and resembles a suitcase.

Whether you use a frame backpack or luggage, if your belongings are cramped, you should try to unpack when you plan to be in one place for a few days. It will give your clothing a chance to air out, and there will be less chance of wrinkling.

Besides your backpack or luggage, you may want to carry a small, light day pack on your trip. On those days when most of your gear can be left behind in a car trunk, tent, or hotel room, a small backpack is useful for carrying lunch, a map and guidebook, and other necessities for an afternoon's outing. Some travelers also pack an empty small, foldable nylon or canvas bag into their luggage, knowing they always come back carrying more than they began with.

How to Pack

When you have cut down what you plan to take until you cannot cut any more, it's time to pack your bag. For ease in finding things, arrange the bag so that all shirts are together, all pants together, and so forth. Socks and underwear can be stuffed into odd corners and empty spaces in your bag, or they can be kept together. You can keep small like items together by using plastic bags or cloth drawstring ditty bags that are easily sewn up.

You may want to make a list of everything you are putting in the luggage. Take one copy of the list along. Check it before you move on from one place to the next. You won't have to rely on your memory to know if your flashlight is missing, and you are more likely to search for (and find) it before it is left behind.

Clothing can be kept fresh and relatively unwrinkled if you are careful. Here are some varied techniques. Experiment to see what works for you.

- Place tissue paper between items of clothing.
- Fold clothing inside out.
- Pack clothing inside plastic cleaner bags.
- Roll clothing.
- Roll clothing into old stockings.
- Put underwear, socks, or stockings into shoes to help the shoes keep their shape.
- Place your most creasable clothing in a suitcase with half of the item hanging over the side. Let pants legs or dress bottoms hang out. Then put the next dress or pair of pants on top of it, this time hanging the bottom over the opposite side. Keep piling the clothing in the suitcase with half of each item draping over the alternate side. When all delicate items are lying in the suitcase, fold the pants legs, shirt sleeves, etc., into the case. Take one from the left, then one from

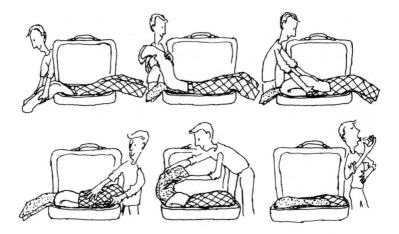

the right, alternating until everything is inside. Since the clothing is not folded with a sharp crease, the crease will not last.

If clothing should wrinkle on the trip, place your garment on a hanger in the bathroom when you take a shower or run bathwater. With the door closed, the steam will probably work out the wrinkles.

You should label every piece of luggage with your name and address. If you do not want strangers to know where you live, use your parents' work address or any other address where the baggage can be returned to you. Another possibility is to use covered luggage tags that hide the information from casual view. Many people put their names on the possessions inside their luggage, too, especially if they are traveling in a group. You may also want to tape some sort of bright symbol (a simple diamond or tic-tac-toe board, for example) on your bags so you can find them easily.

Before you close your luggage and start on your trip, check one more time. Is there something you can remove? Is there anything else you'll need? If the answer to both these questions is no, zip up and get going.

9. On the Trip

This chapter offers hints for enjoying yourself on your vacation: How to eat well without spending too much, how to stay well on the road, and ways to keep your spirits up away from home. Also included are ideas for emergencies.

Eating on a Trip

Next to lodging, food is the most costly vacation expense. Yet it's even more important than usual to eat well when you travel, so that you have the stamina to make good judgments. The solution? Eat regularly but try to save money on meals.

You can lower your food costs by staying out of restaurants for at least one meal a day. It's simple to prepare breakfast in a motel. You can carry cereal along and go out for rolls and milk in the morning, or you can store milk overnight in a sinkful of ice.

If you prefer to prepare lunch or dinner, you may want to eat as you travel. Stop when you are ready and buy food at local markets. You can eat what you buy on trains, planes, and in cars, but it's more refreshing to stop for a while. Your meal at a park or roadside picnic site gives you a chance to get up and move about, often in a picturesque setting. Most rest stops and parks offer running water and bathrooms; some provide barbecue grills.

Many travelers look forward to their visits to local groceries and supermarkets. They view the stops as part of regional sightseeing—an opportunity to try snapper in Seattle, lox in New York, cheese in Wisconsin, and potato rolls in Pennsylvania Dutch country.

When you shop for food, keep in mind the fact that market prices vary. You will usually pay more for an item in a small, 24-hour convenience store than in a supermarket. If you plan to be in one area for more than a day, you might want to check newspaper ads for food sales.

The more you plan to furnish your own meals, the more equipment you will want to bring: thermos, heating coil, cooler, instants—soup, cocoa, coffee. You may want a vegetable peeler, can opener, flatwear (metal or plastic), plates and cups (plastic or paper), and napkins. Some travelers bring along a plastic tablecloth so that the recent history of the picnic table needn't concern them.

When you do eat in restaurants on your trip, you can still do it inexpensively. Here are some hints:

- Eat your big meals as breakfast or lunch, when prices are lower and protein-filled, nutritious specials are often offered.
- Ask the waiter or waitress for the day's specials.
- Read the menu carefully before you order. See what is included with your meal. Are drinks extra?
- Compare menu prices on simple items that you know from your hometown. Is a grilled-cheese sandwich much more or less than you're used to paying?
- Look for smorgasbord restaurants. You can fill up and eat lightly for the rest of the day. Smorgasbord meals are particularly good buys for lunch.
- Try to get a look at the size of portions before you order if you are concerned about being hungry after your meal.
- Ask for your cold drinks without ice.
- Eat regularly and healthfully so that you avoid wasteful spending and caloric binging on fast foods that are costly for what you get.

Whether you eat in restaurants or prepare your own food, try to keep to a balanced diet, including enough vitamins, minerals, proteins, starches, and fiber. Drink plenty of liquids.

Make sure whatever you eat is unspoiled. If it's cooked, see that it's fully cooked. In some foreign countries, tap water is not treated for purity. Check with a travel agent or the consulate to see if this is so where you are going.

If it is, you must take special precautions to avoid bacterial infection and diarrhea. These measures usually include using bottled liquids or boiling the water. You must use bottled or boiled water for drinking, cooking, and even brushing your teeth. Other measures include eating raw fruits and vegetables only if you can peel off the skins, and restricting yourself to higher-quality restaurants.

Tipping in Restaurants

Most restaurants in the United States expect diners to leave a tip for service over and above the cost of the meal. Sometimes 10 or 15 percent is added to your restaurant bill as a mandatory fee for service. In Italy, you pay *pan' e coperto*, a small cover charge for bread. In addition, you are expected to leave a tip. In many parts of Europe a service charge is included in the bill. Most restaurants in the United States, though, do not impose a service or bread surcharge, leaving the choice entirely to the customer instead. Diners traditionally put some money on the table at the end of the meal. Waiters and waitresses depend on tips for a large portion of their livelihood.

In the United States at the present time, a customary tip is 15 to 20 percent of what the total food and drink bill

amounts to, before adding taxes. State taxes vary. If your tax on restaurant meals is about 8 percent, you many find it simple to compute the tip by doubling the tax: 8 percent × 2 = 16 percent, a fine tip.

A Sample Restaurant Meal

cup of soup	$ .80
burger and fries	2.60
drink	.60
Total	4.00
Tax @ 8%	.32
Tip @ 15%	.60
Tip@ 16% (8% × 2)	.64

When you eat with friends, ask the waiter or waitress to give you separate checks. It's easier to figure out what you owe.

Some say the word "tips" stands for "to insure prompt service." If you do not get good service, what should you do? Suppose you haven't gotten your salad. Speak to the waiter and ask for your salad again. If that doesn't help and courses are turtle-slow in coming (or don't come at all), speak to the manager. You may also want to show your displeasure by lowering the tip. Another way to express your feelings is to fill out the customer opinion card some restaurants provide.

Of course, if service has been extra special—prompt, personal, and friendly—you may want to tip more than usual, because a satisfying meal leaves everyone feeling content.

Feeling Good

From time to time when you travel, you may find yourself lonely or anxious. This can happen even if you are with your family or friends. It happens because going on vacation is really making an exchange. You give up the familiar in exchange for adventure and new experiences. If you think about it, you are giving up a good deal. You lose the comforts of your home—your bed, most of your clothes, familiar foods, schedules, and people you can rely on. You can also have feelings of loss if your trip is disappointing—you may be away too long, the weather may be poor, you may not have met the people you'd hoped to see or had the fun you'd wanted. Just giving up the fantasy of the world's greatest vacation and settling for a good time involves a loss.

Even if your trip is everything you'd hoped it would be, you still have to adjust to the new and unexpected. Going from bed to bed and traipsing through cities where you don't know a soul can wear you out. It can make you long for home, or at least give you irritable moments.

What can you do about this problem? First, it helps just to know that some unhappiness is a possibility when you separate yourself from the familiar. Some people may feel low right after leaving, and the feeling passes within a day or two. Other people may suddenly feel empty somewhere in the middle of the trip, and still others tend to get the blues as the return home gets closer.

There are many ways you can help yourself with the tensions and loneliness of travel. Before you leave, perhaps you'd like to pack something from home to take along—a radio, a stuffed animal, a decorative ornament, a letter from a previous trip, such as camp.

On the trip, you can also help yourself through rough times. Ease your sadness by making contact with friends and family left behind. Write a long letter and visualize the image of the recipient reading it. Splurge on a call and talk about your loneliness. Sometimes just discussing it gives you the strength to go on.

Another way to help with lonely or tense times is to give yourself a treat. This might be the time for that expensive dinner or evening's entertainment. You might look for foods like those you get at home, or try to see a movie filmed in your part of the country.

With experience you will learn what style of travel is right for you. You'll find out how long you are comfortable being away. You'll discover if you need to bring small pieces of home (your own pillow, robe, or slippers, for example). You'll learn how often it feels good to call home and how to arrange it. And you'll learn where and how to meet people safely on the road.

Coping with Another Language

When you are in another country, you can cope with the foreign language if you view it as a challenge. Even if you haven't taken a short, intensive course in the language, don't be ashamed—use all of your resources and you'll have fun.

Here are some ideas:
- Learn a few key phrases before you leave, and carry a phrase guide or dictionary.
- Read pictures on stores to know what's sold there.
- Draw your own pictures to tell others what you want. Hold out your map for instructions.
- Gesture. Point.
- Develop your memory. Once you figure out what the word for "street" is, for example, you'll recognize it on a sign next time.
- Keep asking what everything is, particularly on a menu.
- Write down any important information you need, such as the name and address of the hotel. Carefully copy the letters as they are written in that country.
- Remember that most of the people you'll meet are compassionate and more than willing to help. A smile is your international language.

Staying Well

Make sure you take along whatever you need for your health. Bring along a simple first-aid kit—aspirin, Band-Aids, gauze pads, antiseptic. Carry an extra pair of glasses and enough of your pills, plus copies of the prescriptions. The prices for replacing them out of town may be very high. The time lost will also be bothersome. If you have any special health problems, you should wear and carry tags or bracelets that signal health professionals of your allergy, diabetes, or other specific problem.

Check to see if your family's insurance policy covers you for travel illness or accident. If it does, carry the name and number of the policy. If it doesn't, you may want to buy some health insurance for the time you're away. Hospitalization insurance is very important, because a stay in the hospital without coverage is very expensive. Your family's insurance company and your travel agent can provide information.

You stand a better chance of staying out of the doctor's office if you sleep and eat regularly on your trip. Don't change the overall daily amount of sleep or food much from what you'd have at home. Some people find small quantities of food and beverage at frequent intervals are more satisfactory than three meals when they are traveling. Watch for dehydration, especially if you are flying frequently or are visiting desert areas. Compensate with extra liquid. If your skin or hair is drying out, moisturizers, bath oils, and cream rinse can help.

If you should get sick or have an accident, you have

several options. If your condition is severe, have someone call the operator on the nearest pay phone; he or she will send an ambulance. If your condition is not as severe but still requires immediate attention, go to a hospital emergency room—ask someone where a hospital is or look for road signs with a big H. If you can wait for treatment, you can use the Yellow Pages or call the operator to find local specialists. Another method is to stop at a pharmacy and ask for recommendations.

If you get sick abroad, the United States consulate or embassy can help. It can also provide a list of English-speaking doctors.

Staying Safe

Besides the *do*s for a good trip, there are some things you should *not do*. Almost all of them concern safety.

Try to avoid turning painful feelings into actions that hurt you. Frantic overeating or excessive dieting fall into this category. So does driving for very long periods or through the night. You probably know that drug use and dealing, especially abroad, can lead to a lot of trouble.

You should not walk extensively through most downtown city areas at night, even in a group. Nor should you explore parks at night. If an area is new to you, get the bus schedules and follow them; don't stand on corners waiting for long periods. If you go downtown, know beforehand how you will park at the theater, concert hall, or disco. Always watch your valuables. Don't absentmindedly put your wallet, jewelry, or camera down anywhere.

Meeting People

You can meet and enjoy new acquaintances on a trip. If you are cautious, you can find adventure and meet people both similar to yourself and very different from you.

Bear in mind a few things as you meet new people.

* Most of the bonds between travelers do not result in lasting friendships. On the road, you may strike up a friendship with someone you wouldn't spend much time with at home. This is acceptable and totally moral, because the bonds are based on different criteria from those you use at home. You might have gotten together simply because you're both from Minnesota and you haven't met anyone from the Midwest in Wyoming this summer. You might be attracted to your new friend because you want to spend time with a native Hawaiian before you leave Maui. You might be together because you find yourselves following each other around the same museums and your other travel mates won't set foot in another. Or you both may just be lonely for someone to talk to. If you don't expect too much, you can enjoy the time as a happy interlude.
* Limit your first meetings with new people only to public places—museums, cafés, gardens, or parks. These places give you an opportunity to start conversation ("What do you think of that painting?"), and they are safe spots for continuing and deepening conversations.

- Go slowly in developing your new friendships, especially if you are alone. (Spend several days together before deciding to travel to the next city and share a room, for example.)
- Do not go off with strangers without knowing who they are and exactly where they are taking you. If you decide to visit the home of a new acquaintance for a meal, it's a good idea to let someone who is traveling with you know the address and phone number where you can be reached. If you are alone, give the hotel concierge the information.
- Pay careful attention to signals and messages that you might erroneously be sending out or receiving. If you notice differences in manners and attitudes between you and your new friend, try to make adjustments before you give or get the wrong impression. For example, in some countries of Latin America and Asia, if women are not traveling under the protection of other family members, they may be regarded as inviting sexual overtures. At the same time, women who lounge bare-breasted on French Riviera beaches should not necessarily be regarded as signaling readiness for sexual liaisons.

A Word about Cults

It is a sad fact of our times that some shady characters are out looking for vulnerable young people—worn-out travelers, lonely students, and runaways are special prey. Among the most dangerous are pimps looking for prospective prostitutes of both sexes and cult members looking for converts. While some pimps and cult members may be recognizable by eccentric clothing and hairstyles, others look like your most wholesome-looking neighbors.

Beware of strangers who approach you. A trained cult member is taught to address potential converts in terms they understand. For example, if you seem to be a camera bug, you might be approached about photography. "What film do you use?" "Do you like the Nikon?" "How does it compare with the Canon?" As the conversation warms up, it may turn to travel. "Are you in Denver alone?" "Would you like to meet people?" Then the clincher: "There's a slide show tonight. I think you'd like the group. Would you like to come?"

Some invitations from strangers may indeed be gestures of legitimate friendliness. Others may not, however, and you must be cautious. Unfortunately, even the brightest, most sophisticated people have been taken in by cults that seem to offer warmth, companionship, and love. A weekend away can turn into years of isolation from your family.

Harsh as this sounds, none of us seems immune to the advanced techniques of cult brainwashing. The cult people are experts at what they do, so we are best off not flirting with those groups to see if we can outsmart them.

Do not get into debates with them on street corners. Do not try to explain or lie about why you won't come out to their retreat. They are highly trained in methods of wearing you down. Instead, keep repeating one simple phrase over and over. "I'm not interested." And walk away calmly.

Sadly, in this case we do well to listen to our mothers who said, "Never go with strangers." It may be just as dangerous at the age of 18, 20, and 30 as it was at 6 and 7. Only the candy is different.

If You Run Out of Money on a Trip

Try to keep track of your money. Know how much money you started with, and try to write down all your daily expenses in a little notebook. That will help you keep track so that you can set aside money for days you know will be expensive. Money won't slip away from you.

If you find yourself running low on money while traveling, take care of the problem before you are out of cash completely. There are several ways you can approach it. A call home can straighten things out. Your family can wire money from one bank to another or to the nearest Western Union office.

If you have a credit card on the trip, the bank issuing it will usually advance small amounts of cash. American Express will also issue cash to you at its offices, most airline offices, and selected motels. You can also get advice at the American embassy and consular offices abroad. Some people hide $100 in traveler's checks in their suitcases as a reserve fund, only to be used in an emergency. Perhaps this is a good idea for you.

If You Get Lost

Everyone gets lost from time to time on a trip. The old saying "Stay calm" has wisdom. The real question is how to stay calm. If you're not sitting, sit down. Take a moment to catch your breath, then breathe deeply. Perhaps most important is believing that by bedtime you will no longer be lost. Imagine yourself out of your jam and on your way, and you will be taking the first step.

Think your situation out slowly and methodically, using any available maps, signs, geographic or astronomic guidelines (e.g., the position of the sun). If maps and other guideposts cannot help and you seem to be in the middle of nowhere, walk or drive to the next town, or at least to the next intersection. There, road signs may connect you back to your map again.

If you want to ask for directions, knowledgeable people are likely to be found in train station kiosks, the chamber of commerce office, and the police station. Other good bets include workers in post offices, gas stations, and grocery or other stores that deliver merchandise.

If you get lost in the woods, you might find this advice from the *Macmillan Illustrated Almanac for Kids* helpful:

- "Climb to a high place, so you can see distances. Look for a landmark you can head for. . . . If you can't figure a way out, stay where you are. On high ground, build a fire. Feed it with green branches and leaves to make smoke. Searchers may then be able to spot you."
- The authors also recommend sending distress signals in threes—three whistles, three shouts, three flashes from a flashlight.
- "If you decide to walk out, follow a road or trail made by humans. Or follow a power line. Or travel downstream."

When Rooms Are Hard to Get

What should you do if you can't find a place to stay? Suppose you've stopped at every motel and scoured the respectable city hotels, and there's not a room available. The tourist homes have turned off their lights; even the mosquitoes have gone elsewhere for the night.

If this happens, you should not sleep at the side of the road or in the park. It's not a good idea to sleep sitting up in a train or bus station, either. In any of these places you could be arrested by the police or, worse, mugged and robbed by troublemakers.

Where *can* you go?

If you're in a college town, you can go to a fraternity or sorority house. Sometimes these groups will give you a room or let you sleep on their lobby couches. (Some travelers always carry a sleeping bag for crashing.)

Try the bus or train station information booth. The people in charge sometimes know of rooms you haven't seen. There may also be a Travelers Aid booth to help you out (such booths are found mostly in larger stations). In Europe, head right to the kiosk. This tiny booth is set up specifically to list and arrange for rooms in homes and hotels.

Other sources of help include the chamber of commerce, houses of worship, the police, and 800 telephone services. Hotlines, even those primarily devoted to other causes, can make recommendations and intervene. Three national hotlines are CONTACT, the National Runaway

Switchboard, and the Travel Phone North America Desk (see appendix for numbers).

Chances are good you won't get into any kind of jam. But whether your trip goes 100 percent smoothly or has some bumps along the way, traveling is great fun. Here's to—

* planning well
* taking care
* and coming home with fine memories.

Have a wonderful time!

Appendices

TRAVEL RESOURCES
Airplane Travel
    Airlines
    Airline Coupon Brokers
    Courier Firms
Automobile Travel
    Motor Clubs and Touring Services
    Rental Car Chains
Boat Travel
Bus Travel
College Tours
Computerized and Last-Minute Fares; Clearinghouses
For Travelers with Medical Considerations
Guesthouse and Bed-and-Breakfast Organizations

Appendices
Hostels
Motels
Organizations and Services
Discount Motel Chains
Outdoor Travel
Bicycling
Camping
Tour Packagers
Train Travel
Travel Exchange and Aid Programs

ANNUAL AND BIENNIAL PUBLICATIONS
BOOKS
HOW TO MAKE A SHEET SLEEPING SACK

Travel Resources

Here is a list of resources for good traveling. The organizations, clubs, and travel chains selected offer information, guidance, and low-cost arrangements.

(NOTE: Phones with area code 1-800- are toll-free numbers—you do not pay long-distance rates for these calls.)

Airplane Travel

Airlines:

Your Yellow Pages lists the companies that serve your area under the heading "Airline Companies." This is a sampling of large and small, domestic and international, companies.

America West Airlines
1-800-247-5692 except AK, HI, TX

Braniff Airways
1-800-272-6433 except AK, HI, TX

Continental Airlines
1-800-525-0280 except AK, HI
HI: 1-800-231-0850

155

Travel Resources

Delta Air Lines
1-800-523-7777

Eastern Airlines
1-800-327-8376 except AK, FL,
HI

Icelandair
1-800-223-5500 except AK, HI

Midway Metrolink
1-800-621-5700

Muse Air
1-800-882-2828

New York Air
1-800-221-9300

Northeastern International
Airways
1-516-467-3200

Northwest Orient
Domestic Flights:
1-800-225-2525
International Flights:
1-800-447-4747

Olympic Airways
1-800-223-1226 except AK, HI,
NY

Pan American World Airways
1-800-221-1111 except AK, HI
AK: 1-800-227-3051

People Express Airlines
Check your telephone directory
for the number in your area.

Pilgrim Airlines
DC, DE, MA, MD, ME, NH, NJ,
NY, OH, PA, RI, VA, VT, WI:
1-800-243-0490
CT: 1-800-282-8568

PSA Airlines
1-800-854-2902 except AK,
CA, HI

Rocky Mountain Airways
AZ, KS, NE, NM, OK, UT, WY:
1-800-525-0175

Royale Airlines
1-800-282-3125 except AK, HI,
LA
LA: 1-800-282-8568

Sabena—Belgian World
Airlines
1-800-362-8050

Sky West Airlines
1-800-453-9417 except AK, HI,
UT
UT: 1-800-662-4237

Tower Air
1-800-221-2500 except AK, HI,
NY

Trans World Airlines
Domestic Flights:
1-800-421-8710
International Flights:
1-800-892-4141 except AK,
HI

United Airlines
Check your telephone directory
for the number in your area.

USAir
1-800-428-4322

Virgin Atlantic Airways, Ltd.
1-212-242-1330

Western Airlines
1-800-227-6105

World Airways
1-800-772-2600

Airline Coupon Brokers:

The Coupon Broker
1780 South Bellaire Street
Suite 125
Denver, CO 80222
1-303-759-1953

Travel Discounts International
155 East 55th Street
New York, NY 10022
1-212-826-6644

Travel Enterprises, Inc.
57 East 11th Street
New York, NY 10003
1-212-533-4440

Courier Firms:

Archer Courier Systems
855 Avenue of the Americas
New York, NY 10001
1-212-563-8800

Stratus Transportation Services
P.O. Box 280235
San Francisco International
Airport
San Francisco, CA 94128
1-415-340-1778

Automobile Travel

**Motor Clubs and
Touring Services:**

Allstate Motor Club
30 Allstate Plaza
Northbrook, IL 60062
1-800-323-6282

American Automobile
Association
1712 G Street N.W.
Washington, DC 20006
1-800-336-4357 for emergency
road service only.
For other business, check your
phone book for the office in
your area.

American Automobile Touring
Alliance
888 Worcester Street
Wellesley, MA 02181

American Express Driver
Security Plan
P.O. Box 9014
Des Moines, IA 50306

Amoco Motor Club
P.O. Box 9014
Des Moines, IA 50306

157

Travel Resources

ARCO Travel Club
P.O. Box 100017
Atlanta, GA 30348
1-800-272-6669

CCI Auto Tape Tours
P.O. Box 385
Scarsdale, NY 10583
1-914-472-5133

Chevron Travel Club
Concord, CA 94524
1-800-227-1306

Exxon Touring Service
P.O. Box 10210
Houston, TX 77206
Check your phone book for an
office in your area, or visit a
nearby gas station.

Exxon Travel Club
4550 Dacoma
Houston, TX 77092
1-413-680-5723

Gulf Auto Club
P.O. Box 105287
Atlanta, GA 30348
1-800-422-2582

Mobil Travel Service
P.O. Box 25
Versailles, KY 40383
Check your phone book for an
office in your area, or visit a
nearby gas station.

National Travel Club
51 Atlantic Avenue
Floral Park, NY 11001
1-516-352-9700

National Travel Tapes
989 East 900 South
Salt Lake City, UT 84105
1-800-641-1531 except UT
UT: 1-801-359-6263

Shell Motorist Club
8500 North Michigan Road
Indianapolis, IN 46268
1-800-621-8663

Texaco Star Club
250 John W. Carpenter
Dallas, TX 75222
1-214-258-2060

Texaco Travel Service
Texaco, Inc.
4800 Fournece Place
Room W106
Bel Air, TX 77401
1-800-348-2022

Travelcassettes
P.O. Box 982
New Haven, CT 06504
1-203-777-8242

Rental Car Chains:

Avis
Check your phone book for
locations near you.
1-800-331-1212

Budget
Check your phone book for
locations near you.
1-800-527-0700

158

Dollar Rent a Car
Check your phone book for
   locations near you.
1-800-421-6868

Europe by Car
One Rockefeller Plaza
New York, NY 10020
1-800-223-1516 except NY
NY: 1-212-581-3040

General Rent-a-Car
3100 South Federal Highway
Fort Lauderdale, FL 33123
1-800-327-7607

Hertz
Check your phone book for
   locations near you.
1-800-654-3131

National Car Rental
Check your phone book for
   locations near you.
1-800-328-4567

Rent-a-Dent
Check your phone book for
   locations near you.
1-800-426-5243

Rent A Wreck
Check your phone book for
   locations near you.
1-800-421-7253

Ugly Duckling Rent-A-Car
Check your phone book for
   locations near you.
1-800-843-3825

Boat Travel

Cruise Line International
   Association
17 Battery Place
Suite 631
New York, NY 10004
1-212-425-7400

Freighter Travel Club of
   America
P.O. Box 12693
Salem, OR 97309
1-503-399-8567

Travltips Cruise and Freighter
   Travel Association
Box 188
Flushing, NY 11358
1-718-939-2400

Windjammer Barefoot Cruises
P.O. Box 120
Miami Beach, FL 33139
1-305-373-2090

Bus Travel

The Green Tortoise
P.O. Box 24459
San Francisco, CA 94124
1-800-227-4766 except CA
San Francisco: 1-415-821-0803
Los Angeles: 1-213-392-1990
(Alternative cross-country bus
   travel, with sleeping
   arrangements)

Greyhound Lines
Greyhound Tower
Phoenix, AZ 85077
Or call your local bus terminal.

159

Travel Resources

Trailways, Inc.
1500 Jackson Street
Dallas, TX 75201
Or call your local bus terminal.

College Tours

Ides of April College Tours
160 West 95th Street
New York, NY 10025
1-212-265-5343

Inter-Collegiate Holidays, Inc.
501 Madison Avenue
New York, NY 10022
1-212-355-4705

Computerized and Last-Minute Fares; Clearinghouses

Access International
250 West 57th Street
New York, NY 10019
1-212-333-7280

Discount Travel International
114 Forest Avenue
The Ives Building, Suite 205
Narberth, PA 19072
1-215-668-2182

Moments Notice
40 East 49th Street
New York, NY 10017
1-800-221-4737 except NY
NY: 1-212-486-0503

Stand-Buys, Ltd.
311 West Superior
Suite 414
Chicago, IL 60610
1-800-621-5839 except IL
IL: 1-800-972-5858

Traveltron
Irvine, CA
1-714-851-8073

Vacations To Go
120 Wall Street
Suite 1044
New York, NY 10005
1-800-624-7338

Worldwide Discount Travel
  Club
1674 Meridian Avenue
Miami Beach, FL 33139
1-305-895-2082

For Travelers with Medical Considerations

Flying Wheels Travel
143 West Bridge
Owatenna, MN 55060
1-800-533-0363
(Tours and information)

Medic Alert Foundation
  International
Department AZ
P.O. Box 1009
Turlock, CA 95380
1-800-344-3226
(Necklaces, bracelets, and cards
identifying ailments, medical
information, and access to
emergency phone numbers)

Society for the Advancement of
Travel for the Handicapped
26 Court Street
Brooklyn, NY 11201
1-718-858-5483

Travel Information Center of the
Moss Rehabilitation Hospital
12th Street and Tabor Road
Philadelphia, PA 19141
1-215-329-5715
(Information only)

Guesthouse and
Bed-and-Breakfast
Organizations

Bed and Breakfast International
151 Ardmore Road
Kensington, CA 94707
1-415-525-4569

The International Spareroom
P.O. Box 518
Solana Beach, CA 92075

Northwest Bed and Breakfast
7707 Southwest Locust Street
Portland, OR 97223
1-503-246-8366

Tourist House Association of
America
R.D. 2, Box 355A
Greentown, PA 18426
1-717-857-0856

Hostels

American Youth Hostels
1332 I Street N.W.
Suite 800
Washington, D.C. 20005
1-202-783-6161
Or check phone directories of
cities near you.

Motels

Organizations and Services:

American Hotel and Motel
Association
888 Seventh Avenue
New York, NY 10019
1-212-265-4506

Discount Motel Chains:

Best Western International
6201 North 24 Parkway
Phoenix, AZ 85016
1-800-528-1234

Budget Host Inns
P.O. Box 10656
Fort Worth, TX 76114
1-817-626-7064

Days Inns of America
2751 Buford Highway
Northeast
Atlanta, GA 30324
1-800-325-2525

161

Travel Resources

Econo Lodges of America
6135 Park Road, Suite 200
Charlotte, NC 28210
1-800-446-6900 except VA
VA: 1-800-582-5882

Family Inns of America
P.O. Box 10
Pigeon Forge, TN 37863
1-800-251-9752

Friendship Inns International
2627 Paterson Plank Road
North Bergen, NJ 07047
1-800-453-4511

Imperial 400 National
1830 North Nash Street
Arlington, VA 22209
1-800-368-4400 except TX
TX: 1-800-252-9649

La Quinta Plaza Motor Inns
P.O. Box 32064
San Antonio, TX 78216
1-800-531-5900

Motel 6
51 Hitchcock Way
Santa Barbara, CA 93105
1-805-682-6666

Red Roof Inns
4355 Davidson Road
Amlin, OH 43002
1-800-848-7878 except OH
OH: 1-800-282-7990

Regal 8 Inns
P.O. Box 1268
Mount Vernon, IL 62864
1-618-242-7240

Scottish Inns
Suite A
1152 Spring Street
Atlanta, GA 30309
1-800-251-1962

Select Inn of America
Box 2603
Fargo, ND 58108
1-701-282-6300

Super 8 Motels, Inc.
P.O. Box 49
Aberdeen, SD 57401
1-800-843-1991

Susse Chalet Motor Lodges
2 Progress Avenue
Nashua, NH 03060
1-800-258-1980 except NH
NH: 1-800-572-1880

Thrifty Scot Motels, Inc.
1 Sunwood Drive
P.O. Box 399
St. Cloud, MN 56302
1-800-228-3222
Nebraska and Canada call
  collect: 1-402-572-7722

Thr-rift Inns
6129 Jefferson Avenue
Newport News, VA 23605
1-804-838-6852

Travelodge
1973 Friendship Drive
El Cajon, CA 92090
1-800-255-3050

Treadway Inns
50 Kenney Place
Saddle Brook, NJ 07662
1-800-631-0182

USA Inns
Travelers' Hospitality
P.O. Box 658
Goodlettsville, TN 37072
1-800-238-2552

Outdoor Travel

Bicycling:

American Youth Hostels
See under hostels.

Bikecentennial
P.O. Box 8308
Missoula, MT 59807
1-406-721-1776
(Nine thousand miles of
researched routes and other
cycling information)

International Bicycle Touring
Society
2115 Paseo Dorado
La Jolla, CA 92037

League of American Wheelmen
(L.A.W.)
P.O. Box 988
Baltimore, MD 21203
(Touring, safety, and hospitality
homes information)

New England Bicycling Center
The Inn at Danbury
Route 104
Danbury, NH 03230
1-603-768-3318

Camping:

Adirondack Mountain Club
172 Ridge Street
Glens Falls, NY 12801
1-518-793-7737

Advisory Service on Camps
18 East 41st Street
New York, NY 10017
1-212-696-0499

American Camping Association
5000 State Road 67 North
Martinsville, IN 46151
1-317-342-8456

Appalachian Mountain Club
5 Joy Street
Boston, MA 02108
1-617-523-0636

Appalachian Trail Conference
P.O. Box 807
Harpers Ferry, WV 25425
1-304-535-6331

Kampgrounds of America, Inc.
P.O. Box 30558
Billings, MT 59114
1-406-248-7444

National Campers and Hikers
Association
7172 Transit Road
Buffalo, NY 14221
1-716-634-5433

National Forest Service
Recreation Department
United States Department of
Agriculture
Washington, DC 20250
1-202-447-3706

Travel Resources

National Parks Service
United States Department of the
  Interior
Washington, DC 20240
1-202-343-4747

Outward Bound
384 Field Point Road
Greenwich, CT 06830
1-800-243-8520

Sierra Club
730 Polk Street
San Francisco, CA 94109
1-415-981-8634

Tour Packagers

*Many of these agencies have
branch offices around the
country. Consult your Yellow
Pages under "Travel
Agencies."*

Ask Mr. Foster Travel Service
7833 Haskell Avenue
Van Nuys, CA 91406
1-800-243-6346

Club Med
3 East 54th Street
New York, NY 10019
1-800-CLUB MED except NY
NY: 1-212-750-1670

Contiki Holidays
1432 East Katella Avenue
Anaheim, CA 92805
1-800-626-0611 except CA
CA: 1-800-624-0611

Earthwatch
10 Juniper Road
Box 127
Belmont, MA 02178
1-617-489-3030

Empress Travel Service
5 Penn Plaza
New York, NY 10001
1-212-563-0560

General Tours
770 Broadway, 10th Floor
New York, NY 10003
1-800-221-2216 except NY
NY: 1-212-598-1800

International Weekends
1170 Commonwealth Avenue
Boston, MA 02134
1-800-468-5000

Liberty Travel
15 A and S Drive
Paramus, NJ 07652
1-201-967-3000

Maupintour
1515 St. Andrews Drive
Lawrence, KS 66044
1-800-255-4266

REL Travel
8 South Third Avenue
Highland Park, NJ 08004
1-800-572-0123 except NJ
NJ: 1-800-458-8822

Train Travel

Amtrak
Office of Consumer Relations
400 N. Capitol St.
Washington, DC 20001
1-800-USA RAIL

Eurailpass Commission
610 Fifth Avenue
New York, NY 10020
1-212-586-0091

Travel Exchange and Aid Programs

American Council for
    International Studies
19 Bay State Road
Boston, MA 02215
1-800-343-7280

American Institute for Foreign
    Study
102 Greenwich Avenue
Greenwich, CT 06830
1-800-243-4567 except CT
CT: 1-203-869-9090

CONTACT Teleministries,
    U.S.A.
Pouch A
Harrisburg, PA 17105
1-717-232-3501
(Referrals for runaways and
    others)

Council on International
    Educational Exchange
205 East 42nd Street
New York, NY 10017
1-212-661-1450

Experiment in International
    Living
Kipling Road
Brattleboro, VT 05301
1-800-451-4465
    except VT
VT: 1-802-257-7751

Harvard Student
    Agencies
Thayer Hall B
Harvard University
Cambridge, MA 02138
1-617-495-9649

Health Care Abroad
923 Investment
    Building
1511 K Street N.W.
Washington, DC 20005
1-202-393-5500

Immunization Alert
P.O. Box 406
Storrs, CT 06268
1-203-487-0422

International Travelers
    Assistance Association
411 Aviation Way
Frederick, MD 21701
1-800-732-5309
    except MD
MD: 1-301-694-6588

National Runaway
    Switchboard
1-800-621-4000

Putney Student Travel
Putney, VT 05346
1-802-387-5885

165

Travel Resources

Servas U.S.
11 John Street
Room 406
New York, NY 10038
1-212-267-0252
(Exchange hospitality in eighty
countries, to promote
goodwill through contact)

TravelCUTS
(formerly Canadian Universities
Travel Service, Ltd.)
44 St. George Street
Toronto, Ontario, Canada
M5S 2E4
1-416-979-2406
(Discounts and tour packages
for Canadian travelers)

Traveler's Aid Association of
America
125 Wilke Road
Suite 205
Arlington Heights, IL 60005
1-312-392-4202

Traveler's Directory
6224 Baynton Street
Philadelphia, PA 19144
(Names of people who share
their homes with travelers—
you can only get the
directory if you're willing to
be listed in it)

Young Men's Christian
Association
356 West 34th Street
New York, NY 10001
1-212-760-5856

Young Women's Christian
Association
National Board
726 Broadway
New York, NY 10003
1-212-614-2700

Youth Exchange
Pueblo, CO 81009
(Directory listing agencies that
sponsor programs for teens)

Annual and Biennial Publications

Birnbaum, Stephen. "Get 'em & Go Travel Guide" series (e.g., *Canada*). Boston: Houghton Mifflin. Yearly.

Bree, Loris G., ed. *State by State Guide to Budget Motels*. St. Paul, Minn.: Marlor Press. Every two years.

Council on International Educational Exchange. *Work, Study, Travel Abroad: The Whole World Handbook*. New York: St. Martin's. Every two years.

Council on International Educational Exchange and Cohen, Marjorie A. *Where to Stay U.S.A.* New York: Frommer/Pasmantier. Every two years.

Crampton Associates, ed. *Airport Transit Guide*. Glen Elyn, Ill.: Paramount Publishing. Annual. (How to get from the airport to the business district.)

Crossette, Barbara, ed. *America's Wonderful Little Motels and Inns*. New York: Congdon & Weed. Yearly.

Eisenberg, Gerson G. *Learning Vacations: A Guide to All Season Worldwide Educational Travel*. Baltimore: Educational Enterprises.

Annual and Biennial Publications

Fodor, Eugene. "Fodor's Budget" series (e.g., *Fodor's Budget Hawaii*). New York: Fodor. Every two years.

———. "Fodor's U.S.A." guides (e.g., *Fodor's Far West*). New York: Fodor. Every two years.

Frommer, Arthur. "Frommer's Dollarwise Guide" series (e.g., *Frommer's Dollarwise Guide to Florida*). New York: Frommer/Pasmantier. Every two years.

———. "Frommer's Guide" series (e.g., *Hawaii on $25 a Day*). New York: Frommer/Pasmantier. Every two years.

———. *How to Beat the High Cost of Travel*. New York: Frommer/Pasmantier. Every two years.

Harvard Student Agencies. "Let's Go" series (e.g., *Let's Go: California & the Pacific Northwest*). New York: St. Martin's. Yearly.

Meadowbrook Reference Group. Economy Motel Guide. Minneapolis: Meadowbrook Press. Every two years.

Miller, Jess. *Directory of On-Campus Lodging for Tourists*. Indian River, Miss.: Jess Miller Publication Company. Yearly.

Mobil Oil. "Lodging for Less" series (e.g., *Eastern States*). Chicago: Rand McNally. Yearly.

Mort. *Mort's Guides to Low-Cost Vacations & Lodgings on College Campuses: USA & Canada*. Princeton, N.J.: C.M.G. Publishing Co.

Rand McNally and Company. *Guidebook to Campgrounds: A Family Camping Directory of Campgrounds throughout the United States and Canada*. Chicago: Rand McNally. Yearly.

———. "Mobil Travel Guide" series (e.g., *Southeastern States*). Chicago: Rand McNally. Yearly.

Stein, Shifra. "Day Trips" series (e.g., *Day Trips: Minneapolis*). (Published by various companies.)

Thaxton, John. *Bed & Breakfast America*. New York: Burt Franklin. Every two years.

Woodall's North American Campground Directory. New York: Simon & Schuster. Yearly.

Books

Books available in paperback editions are marked *.

*Adler, Jack. *The Consumer's Guide to Travel.* Santa Barbara, Cal.: Capra Press, 1983.

America Magazine, eds. *Road Notes: A Student's Guide to North American Adventures and Delights.* Chicago: Rand McNally, 1981.

*Arnold, Bob. *Discount America Guide's Special Budget Travel Edition.* New York: Discount America, 1983.

*Bairstow, Jeffrey. *Four Season Camping.* New York: Random House, 1982.

Barich, Bill. *Traveling Light.* New York: Viking, 1984.

*Berg, Rick. *The Art and Adventure of Traveling Cheaply.* New York: New American Library, 1981.

*Bodin, Fredrik. *How to Get the Best Travel Photographs.* Somerville, Mass.: Curtin and London, 1982.

*Bree, Marlin, and Bree, Loris. *Affordable Travel.* St. Paul, Minn.: Marlor Press, 1983.

*Bridge, Raymond. *Bike Touring: The Sierra Club Guide to Outings on Wheels.* San Francisco: Sierra Club Books, 1979.

Books

*Browder, Sue. *The American Biking Atlas and Touring Guide.* New York: Workman, 1974.

Calder, Jean. *Walking: A Guide to Beautiful Walks and Trails in America.* New York: Morrow, 1977.

Campus Travel Service. *United States and Worldwide Travel Accommodation Guide.* (College stays) Newport Beach, Cal.: Teacher's Tax Service, n.d.

*Carlson, Raymond, ed. *National Directory of Budget Motels,* rev. ed. Babylon, N.Y.: Pilot Books, 1984.

*————. *National Directory of Free Vacation and Travel Information,* rev. ed. Babylon, N.Y.: Pilot Books, 1984.

*————. *National Directory of Low-Cost Tourist Attractions.* Babylon, N.Y.: Pilot Books, 1979.

*Celebrity Publishing, Inc. *Toll-Free Travel-Vacation Phone Directory.* Suffern, N.Y.: Celebrity Publishing, 1982.

*Colby, C. B., ed. *Camper's and Backpacker's Bible.* South Hackensack, N.J.: Stoeger, n.d.

*Cranfield, Ingrid, ed. *The International Travelers' Handbook.* New York: Doubleday, 1983.

*Cuthbertson, Tom. *Anybody's Bike Book,* 3rd rev. ed. Berkeley, Cal.: Ten Speed Press, 1984.

Dickerman, Patricia. *Adventure Travel.* Stockbridge, Mass.: Berkshire Traveller Press, 1983.

Dolan, Edward F., Jr. *Bicycle Touring and Camping.* New York: Messner, 1982.

*Ehret, Charles, and Scanlon, Lynne W. *Overcoming Jet Lag.* New York: Berkley, 1983.

*Elman, Robert, with Rees, Clair. *The Hiker's Bible,* rev. ed. New York: Doubleday, 1982.

*Farlow, Susan. *Made in America: A Guide to Tours of America's Workshops, Factories, Farms, Mines, and Industries.* New York: Hastings, 1979.

Fletcher, Colin. *The New Complete Walker III.* New York: Knopf, 1984.

George, Jean Craighead. *The American Walk Book.* New York: Dutton, 1979.

Grimes, Paul. *The New York Times Practical Traveler.* New York: Times Books, 1985.

*Hargrove, Penny, and Liebrenz, Noelle. *Backpacker's Sourcebook,* 2nd ed. Berkeley, Cal.: Wilderness Press, 1983.

*Jacobson, Cliff. *Canoeing Wild Rivers.* Merrillsville, Ind.: ICS Books, 1984.

Kaye, Dena. *The Traveling Woman.* New York: Bantam, 1981.

Kemsley, William, ed. *The Whole Hiker's Handbook.* New York: Morrow, 1979.

Kinney Shoes. *Walking Tours of America.* New York: Kinney Shoes, n.d.

*McGough, Elizabeth. *On Your Own in Europe: A Teen-Agers' Travel Guide.* New York: Morrow, 1978.

*Mitchell Beazly Pub. Ltd. *The Pocket Medical Encyclopedia and First Aid Guide.* New York: Simon & Schuster, 1979.

*Nineham, Gillian, ed. *Adventure Holidays 1985.* Cincinnati: Writer's Digest, 1984.

*Parker, Gail R. *Holidays for One: Vacations for the Solo Traveler.* Fairfield, Cal.: PS Publications, 1981.

Reamy, Lois. *Travelability: A Guide for Physically Disabled Travelers in the U.S.* New York: Macmillan, 1978.

*Rice, William, and Wolf, Benton, eds. *Where to Eat in America,* rev. ed. New York: Random House, 1979.

*Riviere, Bill. *The Camper's Bible,* 3rd rev. ed. New York: Doubleday, 1984.

Riviere, William, and L. L. Bean Staff. *The L. L. Bean Guide to the Outdoors.* New York: Random House, 1981.

*Roberts, Harry. *Movin' On: Equipment and Technique for Winter Hikers,* rev. ed. Boston: Stone Wall Press, 1977.

*Rundback, Betty, and Kramer, Nancy. *Bed and Breakfast U.S.A.: A Guide to Tourist Homes and Guest Houses.* New York: Dutton, 1985.

*Scheller, William G. *Train Trips: Exploring America by Rail,* rev. ed. Charlotte, N.C.: East Woods Press, 1984.

Shemanski, Frances. *A Guide to Fairs and Festivals in the United States.* Westport, Conn.: Greenwood Press, 1984.

Books

————. *A Guide to World Fairs and Festivals.* Westport, Conn.: Greenwood Press, 1985.

*Simony, Maggy, ed. *Traveler's Reading Guides: Background Books, Novels, Travel Literature, and Articles.* Vol. 1 *(Europe)* 1981; Vol. 2 *(North America)* 1982; Vol. 3 *(Rest of the World)* 1984. Bayport, N.Y.: Freelance Publications Limited.

Sloane, Eugene A. *The All New Complete Book of Bicycling,* rev. ed. New York: Simon & Schuster, 1983.

Sparks, Lee, ed. *Youth Group Travel Directory.* Loveland, Colo.: Group Books, 1983.

*Specialty Travel Index Publishers. *The Adventure Vacation Catalog.* New York: Simon & Schuster, 1984.

Stewart, Marjabelle Young. *Marjabelle Stewart's How to Travel Book for Teens.* New York: McKay, 1981.

*Swanson, Jack, and Karsh, Jeff. *Rail Ventures.* Ouray, Colo.: Wayfinder Press, 1982.

Tobey, Peter, ed. *Two Wheel Travel: Bicycle Camping and Touring.* New York: Dell, 1973.

Tourist House Associates of America. *Guide to Guest Houses and Tourist Homes U.S.A.* Greentown, Pa.: Tourist House Associates of America, Inc., n.d.

*Urban, John. *White Water Handbook for Canoe and Kayak.* Boston: Appalachian Mountain Club, 1981.

VanMeer, Mary. *Free Attractions, USA.* Santa Fe: John Muir Publications, 1984.

*VanMeer, Mary, ed. *Free Campgrounds, USA,* rev. ed. Charlotte, N.C.: East Woods Press, 1983.

*Wallace, William W. *Pocket Books Guide to National Parks.* New York: Pocket Books, 1984.

Weiss, Louise. *Access to the World: A Travel Guide for the Handicapped.* New York: Facts On File, 1983.

*Wirth, Bob. *Backpacking in the Eighties.* Englewood Cliffs, N.J.: Prentice-Hall, 1984.

*Zussman, Mark. *Make Friends While Traveling.* Tenafly, N.J.: Symphony, 1983.

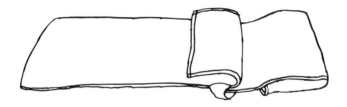

How to make a sheet sleeping sack:

AYH recommends choosing lightweight material—nylon or cotton is good for easy packing. Their instructions: "Sew the bag to measure 78 in. long × 30 in. wide with a pocket to cover the pillow 18 in. deep. A flap of 24 in. is needed on top to protect the upper blanket, and a gusset on each side of the bag adds roominess and prevents tearing."

Index

Numbers in *italics* indicate appendix references.

Index

Index

Index